THE WAY IT WAS

To Elizabeth
From Ken
with christian greetings

THE WAY IT WAS

Ken Walters

Terra Nova Publications

First published by Terra Nova Publications Ltd, 2003

Published in Great Britain by
Terra Nova Publications Ltd
PO Box 2400, Bradford on Avon, Wiltshire BA15 2YN

Scripture quotations taken from the
HOLY BIBLE, NEW INTERNATIONAL VERSION.
Copyright © 1973, 1978, 1984 by International Bible Society.
Used by permission of Hodder and Stoughton Ltd.*
All rights reserved.
[*See notes, for list of NIV quotations.]

ISBN 1 901949 25 7

Cover design by Gazelle Creative Productions.
Cover photograph:
SHEPHERDS FIELDS BETHLEHEM
where the angel of the Lord appeared to them
heralding the birth of Jesus.
A KEITH ELLIS PICTURE
Keith Ellis ARPS, Bible*Lands*.

Printed in Great Britain by
Bookmarque Ltd, Croydon, Surrey

Contents

Acknowledgments

I have had the privilege of a reasonably successful life in science and I have been blessed with very congenial colleagues and friends, both within and outside the University of Wales. I have been associated with that university for fifty years, first as a student at the University of Wales Swansea and then as a member of the Mathematics Faculty at the University of Wales Aberystwyth. As I recall the comings and the goings over all those years, I am reminded of the words of the psalmist: "The boundary lines have fallen for me in pleasant places; surely I have a delightful inheritance", and I am happy to acknowledge the importance of a strong Christian faith over all those years. I would particularly like to put on record how much I have appreciated being associated with St Michael's Parish Church, Aberystwyth, during the last twenty five years. The church has seen significant growth and blessing over those years, first through the pioneering ministry of The Reverend Bertie Lewis and then through the dynamic leadership and inspired preaching of The Reverend Canon Stuart Bell. Over the last ten years, I have had the privilege of serving St Michael's, first as People's Warden and then, more latterly, as Rector's Warden.

Over the years, I have often been asked to preach at the Sunday services at St Michael's, and I am indebted to one of the church members, the late Noel Butler, who encouraged me to contemplate writing up my sermons in book form. To do this in any complete sense would not have been feasible, but there was a subset of messages, which seemed appropriate for dissemination, most of which have involved preaching as if one of the leading players in the unfolding Gospel story. In these, I have tried to place myself in the characters' streams of consciousness. Hence this collection, offered as *The Way it Was*.

During the preparation of the original sermons, I had access to a number of very helpful commentaries and Christian classics in my extensive library, and I may have used a sentence here and there from these helps, without being able to make specific acknowledgment. I have naturally retained as much of the original sermons as possible in the chapters of this book and, for obvious reasons, therefore, I shall simply acknowledge collectively my indebtedness to the writings of such scholars and interpreters as William Barclay, F. F. Bruce, C. H. Dodd, Michael Green, C. S. Lewis, Martyn Lloyd Jones, F. B. Meyer, Campbell Morgan, C. H. Spurgeon, John Stott, M. C. Tenney, Leslie Weatherhead and Alexander Whyte.

I should like to express my deep gratitude to my university secretary and Christian friend, Mrs Pat Evans, who has carried out the typing and related activities with her customary skill and good humour. I should also like to acknowledge the encouragement and helpful advice of my college C.U. colleague and long-time friend, The Reverend Geraint Fielder.

As the text of *The Way it Was* was evolving, I had many reasons to seek the advice of Mary, my wife of over forty years, and I am happy to express again my love for her and my indebtedness to her, both within the university sphere and particularly in our joint Christian enterprises. One of the hymns sung at our wedding was, "How good is the God we adore" and if, after reading this book, you are encouraged to echo such sentiments, I shall be satisfied.

Foreword

By The Reverend Canon Stuart R. Bell,
Rector of St Michael's Parish Church, Aberystwyth

I heard about the 'preaching professor' long before I came to the parish of Aberystwyth. A friend had attended a service in St Michael's, and the theme of the sermon preached by Ken Walters was 'On Eagles' Wings', which was also the title of a new music cassette recorded by the worship group. My friend was impressed by what he heard. Now, more than twenty years later, along with other members of our congregation, I still have the benefit of listening to Ken and enjoying his stimulating preaching, which has thrilled and taught many, and under which some have been converted.

Ken has a style which is unusual for a preacher. We never have three points, nor the verse by verse analysis of a text, but rather he begins with a captivating introduction and then simply develops his theme until he has finished. Much of it centres on careful research of the story line or the character, and the theme always comes alive under his hand.

There is the logic of a university mathematics professor in our pulpit, but also the warmth of heart of a godly man who has done more than just thought about his subject. The theme comes from his soul, which was touched by God so many years ago, and which goes on being touched by God regularly, simply because he is constantly open to the Holy Spirit.

As you read this book, which is based on some of the sermons that have already blessed our congregation in St Michael's, Aberystwyth, so you will be blessed, too. That much is guaranteed.

Stuart R. Bell

Prologue

This book contains my own meditative reflections in the style of 'first person narrative'. However, in the story–telling, I have made every effort to ensure that nothing I have written is contrary to Holy Scripture, which I believe to be God's only self revelation to man.

My intention has been to whet the appetite of the reader for personal devotional study of the Bible. My great desire has been to stimulate and encourage others to search the Scriptures for themselves. Please read *The Way it Was* as flowing from my personal response to the Lord Jesus Christ, and my desire to tell others about him. This book is offered as an encouragement to look at the claims he made about himself and the facts concerning his life, death and resurrection, as recorded in the Gospels, and the claims others made about him, as recorded in the Acts of the Apostles and the Epistles.

Ken Walters
Aberystwyth

1

The Baptist

I write from a fortress, one of a number Herod the Great built during his wicked reign. This one is at Machaerus, in dark and rugged country to the east of the Dead Sea. The fortress is over one thousand metres above the sea and we are cut off from the rest of the world. There are no roads here, only narrow paths; these lead all the way up from the Jordan Valley to this bare and desolate region that people call Moab.

I am not here by choice. I am a prisoner of Herod Antipas, that infamous son of an infamous father. Antipas is his father's son in so many ways —weak, cruel, sensual, ostentatious, shallow. I have heard him called a fox. Out of the window I can just make out the fertile Jordan valley, which has so many memories for me. But I am rushing ahead. Let me go back to the beginning.

My parents were old when I was conceived, way past the normal age of child bearing, and people saw my birth as a miracle. You may have heard of my parents. My father, Zechariah, was a priest. My mother's name was Elizabeth; both of them could claim to be descendants of Aaron, who is well known in the history of my people.

My parents certainly saw my birth as a miracle, and my father often recounted the strange, even bizarre, events that surrounded it. He was left in no doubt that the child would be a son, and should be called John, which means 'the grace and mercy of God; Jehovah has been gracious' —very appropriate in the circumstances!

Then it seems that my father was struck dumb —for a lengthy period. The neighbours expected me to be called Zechariah, after my father of course, but he made it quite plain at my birth, using a writing tablet, that I was to be called John, and at that very moment his voice returned. All very strange, certainly, and it left the whole neighbourhood awestruck. It must have been an interesting time!

My father had been made aware that the whole event was to be somewhat unusual. I was not to take any wine. I was to be a so-called 'Nazarite', with an unusual lifestyle, but the promise given to my father was more than compensation —I would, in due course, bring many back to the Lord their God. I would somehow have the spirit and power of Elijah, that great prophet. I would prepare the people for something momentous, which would come from the Lord.

My mother was not left out either. She had an unusual meeting with another pregnant woman called Mary. She was a cousin, and it seems that she stayed with my parents for about three months. Apparently, the meeting between Mary and my mother was charged with spiritual emotion. There was a strong conviction that Mary's child would also have a special ministry. About six months after I was born, Mary gave birth to a son, whom they called Jesus. But that was a long time ago. In fact, over thirty years have passed since then.

But these unusual stories were related to me on so many occasions, and they began to mould my lifestyle. Subconsciously, I began to fashion myself on that great prophet Elijah, which is not too surprising, I suppose.

So I grew up to the east of the river Jordan, in the home of a priest. I had the usual Jewish education and I faithfully observed the Nazarite vow. In due course, both my parents died, when I was still comparatively young.

Inevitably, inexorably, I withdrew from society and retreated to the deserts that surround the Dead Sea. In many ways, I didn't seem to have much alternative —the circumstances of my formative years were, in part, outside my control. Some people said that I deliberately modelled myself on what I knew of the prophet Elijah. There I was with uncut Nazarite locks, a rough haircloth garment as a covering and a leather belt. My diet was basically made up of locusts and wild honey. You will know that locusts and similar morsels were only eaten by the very rich or the very poor. To the rich, they could be a delicacy; to the poor they could be the difference between life and death by starvation.

Anyway, I spent my early years of manhood in the wilderness of Judea, which was the haunt of hermits and the hunting ground of bandits. I studied the Scriptures avidly and I particularly took to myself two passages from the prophets. One was from Malachi, "See, I will send you the prophet Elijah before that great and dreadful day of the LORD comes." Could that apply to me perhaps?

And then there was Isaiah, 'A voice of one calling: "In the desert prepare the way for the LORD; make straight in the wilderness a highway for our God. Every valley shall be raised up, every mountain and hill made low; the rough ground shall become level, the rugged places a plain. And the glory of the LORD will be revealed, and all mankind together will see it. For the mouth the LORD has spoken.""[1] These words burned in my heart. They seemed to be peculiarly for me. I slowly began to see that a focal point of my future ministry would be a preparing of the way for some great event. The imagery was well known to me. Conquerors would send before them a herald, to ensure that the conquered would prepare an approach —a kind of king's highway. Valleys had to be filled up and hills levelled —poetically speaking, of course. So I saw myself as a voice crying in the wilderness, making the paths straight, waiting for the glory of the Lord to be revealed.

But I was, in one sense, conditioned by the normal expectations of my upbringing. The period from my mid twenties had to be a kind of probationary period. It was difficult to do anything dramatic before the age of thirty, but my people felt that by that point manhood had reached its perfection, and I felt free to fulfil my destiny.

I began to understand that the Isaiah passage was indeed for me. I had a strong inner conviction that I was being commissioned by God, and that the word of God was somehow within me, trying desperately to get out. I suppose that is what all the prophets would have felt. I had plenty of time for meditation and questioning. Would God save Israel now, in my day? Would he destroy sin, the fount of all evil? Had the Messiah already come, as my parents had often said? And, all the time, there was the conviction that I needed to step out.

But what an unpromising set of circumstances! No synagogue, no ready congregation, none of the usual advantages of the preacher —only the wilderness of Judea and the banks of the Jordan, and that was where I decided to start preaching —on the river bank, near a ford at a convenient spot, where the river was only just over a half a metre deep and about thirty metres across, except at times of flooding. The surroundings were certainly lush, and in striking contrast to the wilderness where I had spent so much of my time.

And the message I felt I needed to bring to the people? Well, it was an unfolding revelation that was given to me a piece at a time. Certainly, preparing a way for the Lord was a recurring theme, although in the early days I did not know the full significance of the message.

But I did know the weaknesses of my fellow Jews, and I continually preached the need for repentance: "Repent, for the kingdom of heaven is near." The people had to say "sorry" to God, and they had to demonstrate openly that change of heart by being *baptised*. So I quickly became known as John the Baptist. But all the time there was the strong conviction that something momentous was about to happen. What it all meant then began to be revealed, and I preached this message: "After me will come one more powerful than I, the thongs of whose sandals I am not worthy to stoop down and untie. I baptise you with water, but he will baptise you with the Holy Spirit."[2] But more of that in a moment.

In many ways, it was an unpromising location and a decidedly unpopular message. But somehow the word spread and the people came, multitudes from Jerusalem and all the land of Judea, to hear the message and, what is more surprising, to receive it gladly. They were happy to give a tangible outward expression to their change of heart, and I baptised many of them in the River Jordan.

The common people came, the high and mighty as well, but my message was the same to all of them. To the outwardly religious Pharisees, I felt led to say that they were like a brood of vipers and that they needed to produce fruit in keeping with repentance. Tax collectors came, and I simply told them not to collect more than they were required to. Soldiers came, and to them I said, "Don't extort money and don't accuse people falsely —be content with your pay."[3]

Many wanted to believe that I myself was the Messiah, and they would readily have unfurled the old standard of the Maccabees. They would have rallied to my side to rid the land of the oppressors. But I told them that I was only a voice crying in the wilderness to prepare the way for the King. And then something happened which was of the utmost importance. The word of God came to me again.

My cousin, Jesus, appeared on the scene. We had never met. He had been living in Nazareth in the north, in the home of a carpenter. I had been here in the south. But he had now made the journey from Galilee to meet me at the Jordan—no mean distance, a hundred kilometres or so.

He wanted to be baptised, and I thought at first that I should try to prevent him. "I need to be baptised by you," I said. But he insisted, so I baptised him.

When he came out of the water, the heavens seemed to open, and I saw the Holy Spirit descending on him like a dove. I heard a voice: "You are my Son, whom I love; with you I am well pleased."[4] I knew then that the Isaiah prophecy was about him.

The revelation was now complete. When I had told the crowd to give attention to Jesus, the words I used had come straight from God: "Look, the Lamb of God!" At that point, I knew without doubt that Jesus was the Son of

God, but the revelation I had was about a lamb, and about his appointment to bear the sins of the world. Most of my listeners knew the story of Abraham and Isaac. Abraham was told to take his only son, and sacrifice him. Isaac had said, "The fire and wood are here, but where is the lamb for the burnt offering?"

"God Himself will provide the lamb," Abraham had replied. He did, of course, much to Abraham's relief and spiritual comfort. And there I was, telling the crowd to look upon this Jesus as a lamb —an offering. "Behold the Lamb." I recall once again those familiar verses from Isaiah, "We all, like sheep, have gone astray... and the LORD has laid on him the iniquity of us all.... he was led like a lamb to the slaughter."[5]

It was awesome. The word of God came to me that day and left me in no doubt that Jesus of Nazareth was somehow, sometime, to be an offering for the sins of all who will repent.

Then some of my disciples went to join Jesus. It was inevitable; I had said that he should increase as I decreased. Not that all my disciples left me —far from it. It would have been naïve to expect all of them to follow. I have a feeling that some of them will still see themselves as my disciples long after my death. They are attracted to the ascetic lifestyle, and would be reluctant to give it up.

So, after that brief encounter, Jesus left to fulfil his own destiny; to build up his own band of disciples; to preach, to teach, to perform miracles, and God seemed to be with him. As for me, my message continued as before, although I now felt I knew how the kingdom would come. I needed to somehow decrease, to allow my cousin to increase.

This was only a few months ago. It all seemed to happen so quickly. But I have not yet explained why I happen to be imprisoned in this fortress. It all revolves around Herod Antipas, who is ruler in these parts. This is the story. Herod was married, but he got involved in an extra marital affair with a certain Herodias, who was the wife of Herod's half brother, Philip—not Philip the tetrarch, but another son of Herod the Great by the same name.

Now on a trip to Rome, Herod got to know Herodias and became attracted to her. He proposed and she accepted. For her, ambition seems to have been as much of a motivation as passion. In fact I need to tell you that neither Herod nor Herodias are young. Herodias already has a daughter by Philip, who is in her late teens. I say that there was ambition as well as passion. You see, Philip was rich but he had not been made an heir to his father's throne as he had expected. He was rich without a royal position.

So Herod Antipas married Herodias and she brought with her a teenage daughter called Salome. You need to know that our law forbids marriage with a sister-in-law, and many in the nation were outraged. In some ways I was the spokesman for the mood of the time, saying to Herod, "It is not lawful for you to have your brother's wife."[6]

You will not be surprised to learn that Herod got into a wild rage, but he could not do too much about it, because he feared the people. You also won't be surprised to learn that Herodias was less than pleased, and that she nursed a grudge against me.

But I felt reasonably secure, although I had just denounced a ruler who was notoriously fickle and cruel.

Something had to be done to appease Herodias, of course, and Herod's own pride for that matter. So they locked me up in this prison at Machaerus. I am frustrated, certainly, but I feel reasonably secure because of Herod's fear of the people. And here I have again much time for reflection and meditation.

From time to time, I have had news of the successful ministry of my cousin, Jesus. People are flocking to hear him in Galilee. He preaches with winsome power. He seems to have powers to perform miracles: the lame walk, the deaf have their hearing restored and even the dead are raised.

His lifestyle is certainly different from the one I am used to and, in some ways, I am perplexed. My disciples have even gone as far as to ask him, "How is it that we and the Pharisees fast, but your disciples do not fast?"[7]

Wanting to be sure of the significance of all that was happening, I sent a message to Jesus: "Are you the one who was to come, or should we expect someone else?"[8] Where did the lamb of God vision which I had received fit into the news I heard from Galilee? I have to tell you that my question was met by firmness by my cousin, but with kindness. He certainly saw me in the context of that scripture from Malachi. Perhaps I needed not so much fresh facts, as a different way of looking at those I already knew.

But I wonder where the ministry of Jesus is leading. I cannot yet see exactly how his destiny as the lamb of God, who is to take away the sin of the world, will be fulfilled. Time will tell!

Anyway, I have to report some unexpected and very worrying developments. It is Herod's birthday and he has just had a sumptuous party, with many guests from far and wide. Rumour has it that the daughter of Herodias disgraced herself by dancing before them all in the most indecent of ways. It also seems that Herod, in a drunken stupor, has offered her up to half his kingdom. I am unreliably informed that, on consulting with her mother, she has asked for my head! So here I am, looking out at the barren wastes of the wilderness of Judea. I can see the river, and even the place where I baptised so many people.

I hear soldiers approaching. Perhaps it was not a rumour after all? How will it all end?

EPILOGUE

The sequel is well known. John the Baptist was beheaded. His head was placed on a salver and paraded before Herodias and Salome. John's disciples came and buried his body. He was the last in a long line of prophets. He was martyred for his testimony and he was buried in the land of Moab.

The story is firmly rooted in secular history. In fact, you will not find the name Salome anywhere in the Bible. We get her name from Jewish historians of the time.

And the sequel? These words are to be found in Luke Chapter 3: "In the fifteenth year of the reign of Tiberius Caesar—when Pontius Pilate was governor of Judea, Herod tetrarch of Galilee... the word of God came to John, son of Zechariah, in the desert."

We read of Tiberius Caesar, Pilate and Herod simply to pinpoint John the Baptist in history. They are historical markers with little other significance. Today, we only know of Herod and the rest because of John and Jesus.

Herod was a sad case. History records his licentious life, his family miseries, his political manoeuvres, his ruinous defeats. It finally records his fall from the throne and his exile. He was reasonably diplomatic during the reign of Tiberius. But he misread mad Caligula. He wanted a royal title, but instead he was deposed, and exiled to Lyon in France. Interestingly, Herodias was happy to share his fate. Perhaps she had no alternative. What of Salome? A small coin was found which has preserved her appearance for posterity. She is there with her husband: "King Aristobulus and Queen Salome". Did she learn manners and good taste as she grew into full womanhood? We do not know. What we do know is that she has kept Hollywood reasonably busy with her story; and Richard Strauss has an opera named after her. But artists and composers only know of her story because her paths crossed those of John the Baptist.

So, Herod, Herodias and Salome are simply signposts to point us to John the Baptist. And John the Baptist is himself a signpost to point us to Jesus. This is his lasting testimony.

There came a man who was sent from God; his name was John. He came as a witness to testify concerning that light so that through him all men might believe. He himself was not the light; he came only as a witness to the light.[9]

2

Pontius Pilate

I was born at a time when the empire was almost at its peak. It was feared by everyone; it had a fighting force second to none. The general standard of living was incredibly high, with central heating and other mod cons coming on tap.

My parents were from the middle classes and they wanted the best for me. I was introduced to political life and when I reached a sufficiently mature age, in fact twenty seven plus, I was given a plum job in one of our crown colonies. I was the envy of my contemporaries, although they did not realise at the time (and neither did I) what I had let myself in for. I was appointed as Caesar's representative and viceroy in Palestine. My official title was procurator. I had powers to govern Judaea, subject only to the governor of Syria and, of course, the emperor.

I was to be based at Caesarea, on the Mediterranean coast —a very fine setting for a foreign posting. By this time I had married Procula, and everything was set for an idyllic lifestyle. I counted without the Jews! From the start they were the bane of my life. I disliked them intensely, although my wife was strangely drawn to their funny ways and religion. Very soon, the Jews and I were at daggers drawn. You may know that we had given these Jews full religious freedom. In fact, we had granted them some unusual concessions. They could not tolerate idols and we went along with this as best we could. However, at the time of my arrival in Caesarea, emperor worship had been foisted on the soldiers. They were told not only to revere the emperor as king, but also to worship him as a god. So they carried on their standards little effigies of Caesar, to which they had to offer adoration.

Now the special privilege granted to the Jews was simply this: we had agreed that idols would not be used in the vicinity of their holy places. Personally, I thought this was ludicrous, so I surreptitiously sent the troops to Jerusalem and ordered that the images be taken into the city at night. Not surprisingly, the Jews were incensed and outraged. Multitudes of them marched all the way from Jerusalem to my base in Caesarea, a distance of some eighty kilometres. They pleaded for an interview. For five days I held out. After all, why should the Roman procurator be intimidated by these Jewish nobodies? But on the sixth day I decided to see them. They pleaded with me on bended knees to remove the idols. This somehow got to me and I ordered the troops to surround them. I threatened them with instant death unless they went home and kept quiet. To my utter amazement, to a man they stretched out on the ground, and declared that death was better than violation of their laws. What a people! What was I to do? What would you have done? So I gave in, and quietly waited for revenge.

My second brush with them was hardly any better. I decided to build an aqueduct to Jerusalem, and to fund the venture I took money from their temple treasury. I argued this way with them: Look, I have your interests at heart. Water is never plentiful in the capital and at feast times it is often very low. So why shouldn't you bear the cost? But they thought differently! They were a devious and shrewd lot. They argued that I was really doing it for Rome's sake — in case we ever had to lay siege to Jerusalem. I am not going to tell you whether they were right or not. The important thing is that the Jews felt that they already paid enough taxes, and riots broke out all over Jerusalem. This time I was not going to bow to their silly nonsense! I could be as stubborn as them. So I disguised my soldiers as peasants, armed them with clubs, and very soon order was restored. I am afraid that casual spectators as well as rioters were killed. But round two to me! I could feel the smouldering flame of resentment, which never really went away. At the same time, my contempt for the Jews deepened. I am telling you all this by way of background.

Quite out of the blue, I got tied up with one of these Jews, who seemed different from the rest. My wife, in particular, made a study of the fellow and became deeply influenced by his teaching. Basically, he was a plebeian worker, a carpenter from Nazareth in Galilee. He had apparently set out on a preaching mission at the age of thirty. He seemed to have unusual powers, and numerous people said that they had been healed by him. As far as I could judge, there was nothing sinister about his teaching. He was obviously acquainted with—and loved—his native land, its lakes, its shores, its mountains. He would use everyday scenes and experiences in his teaching. The one thing that really appealed to me about him above all else was the fact that the rulers of the Jews hated him! So I assumed he must have something going for him! His name was Jesus.

One night, at Passover time, Procula and I were staying in Jerusalem. We got wind of some suspicious goings on, involving the Jewish rulers and this man Jesus. They had apparently arrested him in a garden near the city, and had taken him to be tried in their own courts. My informants told me that the charges against him were rigged, but that there was no doubt they would get their man. Indeed, if I had not been in Jerusalem at the time, they would have killed him themselves, there and then, as they did one of his followers some time later. (I believe his name was Stephen.) But since I was in the city they needed my countersignature, and they knew it.

I knew that there were a number of inconsistencies in what was going on. The Jewish trial was illegal from beginning to end. I had made a study of their law and I was appalled at their hypocrisy. You see, according to their laws, capital trials could only commence in daytime. They also had to be concluded during daytime. If the prisoner were found guilty, judgment had to be delayed to a second day. What is more, their law said that trials could not be held on the eve of a sabbath or on the eve of a festival. How hypocritical can you get? Can you wonder why I was less than helpful when one of my household slaves told me that the high priest was at the door. Not that he had come into the praetorium of course! It was Passover time, and the Jews regarded all our Gentile homes as unclean. To come in would have defiled them for a full seven days, and their Passover celebrations would have been ruined. So they stayed outside, and I had to go out to them. I began by asking the obvious question: "What charges are you bringing against this man?"[1]

I may have been a little curt, but I was taken aback by the response: "If he were not a criminal, we would not have handed him over to you."

Some people believe that Caiaphas and I had already had a little meeting of minds, and that I had agreed to rubber stamp the whole thing. They believe that my wife's concern for the man had got to me, and I had reneged on the agreement. Don't you believe it! If the Jews were expecting a rubber stamp, they had come to the wrong person, especially in view of the difficulties they had caused me. "Take him yourselves and judge him by your own law," I said.[2]

"But we have no right to execute anyone," was their response. "We have found this man subverting our nation. He opposes payment of taxes to Caesar and claims to be Christ, a king."[3]

So I turned and asked Jesus whether he was the king of the Jews. I well recall His answer: "My kingdom is not of this world.... My kingdom is from another place."[4] Then he said that I was right in saying that he was a king.

I must admit to feeling that I was in the presence of someone who was different, almost larger than life. There was a detachment, a nobility, almost a superiority, perhaps a divinity. I must also admit to being moved, to feeling disturbed —yes, and a little fearful! So I went to the Jews outside and told them that I could find no fault in him.

At this point they changed their tack. "He stirs up the people all over Judea by his teaching. He started in Galilee and has come all the way here."[5] There it was —

something to get me off the hook. They mentioned Galilee, which was under the jurisdiction of King Herod. So I sent him to Herod! I was passing the buck, or so I thought. But this Jesus was no ordinary man, and Herod sent him back to me —a little the worse for wear, but with nothing accomplished. An unhelpful interlude, certainly, but at least Herod and I got on better after that. But what to do with Jesus? I went out again to the Jews and told them that I found no fault in him, and that I was going to punish and then release him. It was not to be as easy as that.

Then I had another brainwave, or so I thought. It was the custom at feast time to release a prisoner to the Jews. So I set Jesus against a notorious criminal named Barabbas: the man of peace against the man of war; all that is good against all that is evil. But to my utter amazement, the crowd chose Barabbas. Now all is clear to me. A murderer he may have been, a scoundrel even, but Barabbas was also a zealot, a freedom fighter. He was obviously popular with a section of the population, long before the chief priests got amongst the crowd. So they chose Barabbas and told me to crucify Jesus. Then something weird happened. My wife sent a message to me, telling me to do nothing to Jesus because he was a just man. She had dreamt about him, which is not really surprising, since she had been slowly coming under the influence of his teaching.

At this point, I symbolically washed my hands and told the crowd that I was innocent of the man's blood. Again, they seemed quite happy to have his blood on them and, indeed, on their children as well.

So I tried one last gamble. I took Jesus and scourged him, which is to say we stripped him to the waist, bound him over a low pillar and beat him until the officer in charge gave a signal to stop. The lashes cut deeply into his back. We then put a kingly robe on him and a mocking crown of thorns on his head. My soldiers were quite indifferent and callous. "Hail, king of the Jews", they shouted. And there he was —a pitiable specimen. In that condition, I presented him to the people again. "Behold the man", I said.

But they wanted his life. I have to admit I grew afraid — not of the Jews, but about the whole business. There he was telling me about myself. He had won the argument in my book, and I again made up my mind to let him go. But the Jews then played their trump card. They knew that Tiberius had become a very jealous ruler. Treason was a crime, an accusation was effectively proof, and proof meant death. So they cried out, "If you let this man go, you are no friend of Caesar...."[6]

In all honesty, I could not risk any further complications at Rome, and I am afraid I deliberately sent this innocent man to his death. My training as a judge told me that Jesus was innocent. My appreciation of human nature told me that Jesus was a just man. My assessment of the Jews told me that they had brought Jesus to me out of envy. I was bored and irritated by the Jews' splitting of hairs and hypocrisy. I am afraid my sense of expediency made me bend to the people's wishes. We nailed his hands and feet to a cross, and he was crucified between two thieves. It all took place so quickly. Eight hours or so after his capture in the garden, he was on the cross.

As you can imagine, I returned to the praetorium to an irate and troubled wife. I had condemned a just man, despite her plea. But I said to her, "Yes, yes, I know. Yes, of course, but what's done is done. It will be all over and forgotten in a fortnight, so don't fret." But it was not all over and forgotten in a fortnight. Even on the day of crucifixion there were strong omens. The sky went as black as pitch, and an eerie calm settled on the city. The Jews insisted that a guard be placed at the tomb of Jesus, in case some of his disciples came and took the body and claimed that he had risen from the dead. At the time, it seemed incomprehensible to me that this motley, fearful and cowardly group of followers could rise to such a devious scheme, but I obliged.

Then, two days later, on the first day of the week, rumours started to circulate that something strange *had* happened. The tomb of Jesus was found empty, and stories started to circulate that this crucified Jesus had been seen alive by some of his followers. There was general disbelief amongst the Jews and it all seemed too far–fetched for me as well, especially as things started to get back to some kind of normality. Then the whole issue surfaced again at another of their feasts, Pentecost. His followers had somehow got a new lease of life and confidence. Their behaviour was quite bizarre, their enthusiasm infectious; they passionately proclaimed the resurrection. Was this the same pathetic bunch which had deserted him at the trial? Apparently, yes! One of them, the worst coward of them all, was evidently preaching with an almost charismatic power, telling all the people that Jesus had indeed been raised from the dead, and that their God was insisting on repentance. I studied very carefully what this man, Peter, was claiming. It went like this: "Men of Israel, listen to this: Jesus of Nazareth was a man accredited by God to you by miracles, wonders and signs. This man was handed over to you by God's set purpose and foreknowledge; and you, with the help of wicked men, put him to death by nailing him to the cross. But God raised him from the dead, freeing him from the agony of death, because it was impossible for death to keep its hold on him."[7]

So we were *all* implicated and guilty, but his disciples were claiming that the cross and resurrection were part of some divine strategy.

The Jews tried to quash the whole thing at the outset, but they had difficulty explaining away the empty tomb and some notable miracles. By this time I had lost the stomach for a fight. Perhaps my wife was right after all! This Jesus was not only a just man but a man sent from God; perhaps the Son of God, as his disciples were making out —and the FIRE SPREAD. We were helpless to interfere. It has apparently reached as far as Rome itself, and it seems that the more the followers of Jesus are persecuted, the more people become his followers.

One of my soldiers, a centurion, came to me after that dreadful day of crucifixion, greatly troubled. "We've killed the Son of God", he said. I now think he was probably right.

In all, I have spent ten years in Judea. All this happened some time ago. Jesus crossed my path for little more than a fleeting moment. I was confronted with greatness and glory, but I chose compromise.

I did go easy on these so—called Christians, but the remainder of my stay in Palestine has been plagued with trouble. At one point, in particular, there was very severe trouble in Samaria, with many assassinations. The Jews have constantly complained to Rome, and, here I am, waiting to hand over power to my successor, Marcellus. I have been summoned to Rome to answer the accusations of the Jews before the emperor.

I wonder what the verdict of history on me will be —a scoundrel, a weakling, a repentant murderer? We shall see! I wonder whether history will even feel I deserve a mention?

RESPONSE

THE APOSTLES' CREED

I believe in God, the Father almighty,
creator of heaven and earth.
I believe in Jesus Christ, his only Son, our Lord.
He was conceived by the power of the Holy Spirit
and born of the Virgin Mary.
HE SUFFERED UNDER PONTIUS PILATE,
was crucified, died, and was buried.
He descended to the dead.
On the third day he rose again.
He ascended into heaven,
and is seated at the right hand of the Father.
He will come again to judge the living and the dead.
I believe in the Holy Spirit,
the holy catholic church,
the communion of saints,
the forgiveness of sins,
the resurrection of the body,
and the life everlasting. Amen.

3

The Jesus File

Come with me to downtown Jerusalem, in the days when Jesus was just about to embark on his public ministry. He had just been baptised by John the Baptist in the river Jordan, and the more discerning of John's disciples had caught the message: "He must increase, but I must decrease." Jesus was clearly the up–and–coming one.

Now in main street, Jerusalem, there was a consultancy firm which specialised in public relations and also, occasionally, head hunting. The firm had a number of satellite offices, including one at Nazareth, a sizeable town in Galilee, some distance north of Jerusalem.

News had reached Jerusalem from Galilee that a second John the Baptist was about to launch out into a public ministry. Now, you need to know that the firm knew all about the ephemeral nature of many new movements. They could recall someone called Judas the Galilean. He had led a revolt, only to be killed, with his disciples scattered. They were now merely a guerrilla movement, trying by fair means and foul to rid the land of Roman domination. They were called Zealots. Then there was John the Baptist, seemingly popular with the people, but preaching a message that was making him unpopular with Herod and the Sanhedrin; so his days could be numbered.

Notwithstanding the vagaries of offering advice and services to mavericks, a young upstart at the office suggested an approach be made to this so–called Jesus of Nazareth. I recently had access to the relevant file. It contained a number of illuminating entries: the first was headed *The Proposal*. I will paraphrase the appropriate minute.

As agreed, I have offered our services to Jesus of Nazareth. He will surely require a group of helpers. I haven't suggested a 'number' to him, but I have emphasised the need for a band of disciples and, in this respect, I have quoted the experiences of his cousin, popularly known as John the Baptist. To whet his appetite, I have made some general suggestions about the makeup of the band; what to look for, what to avoid, and that sort of thing. Here are some of the issues I raised, some pointers for him.

1. Avoid being too parochial. You are from Galilee, so make sure that you have representatives from the surrounding regions like Judea, Peraea, Decapolis and even Samaria. Don't be insular.

2. Include at least one influential Pharisee —to give the band respectability. At the same time, avoid eccentrics, especially those with strong political tendencies. Zealots are certainly out.

3. Don't make the group too intellectual and

learned, but at the same time, avoid those who are brain–dead. In this context, a little learning is *not* a dangerous thing.

4.   Study carefully the personalities and demeanours of all the likely candidates. They have to interact with each other, day in, day out, and personality clashes can be very, very, damaging. There are potential dangers in appointing relatives, and especially sets of brothers. This can generate a potential 'clique' mentality.

5.   As a general rule, avoid appointing too many from the same background and interests, i.e. not too many fishermen and certainly no tax collectors, unless you want a disaster on your hands.

We will be only too happy to assist in the selection process and arrange to interview an agreed shortlist with your good self. We also run courses for new disciples. You will find our terms competitive.

Yours etc.

Now it seems that the offer of assistance was *not* taken up. Indeed, the next file entry is dismissive, written a few months after the first. It is headed *Our Proposal Rejected.* I quote again:

To say that our advice wasn't heeded would be an understatement. It seems that twelve disciples have been chosen by Jesus of Nazareth—all the evidence is that they were hand picked by him; no-one else was involved; they were his choice —and what a choice! Here, we have a classic case of schoolboy howlers —a clear recipe for disaster. You can use this minute in training courses for new members of our office staff, but it is probably too outrageous for that purpose.

I shall list just a few obvious mistakes.

1. Of the twelve who have been chosen, eleven are from Galilee. The odd one out is a Judas Iscariot, who hails from Judea.

2. Five of the twelve are from the same village in Galilee, called Bethsaida. They are named Simon, Andrew, James, John and Philip. At least four of them are fishermen, having apparently worked together in the same business.

3. There are at least three sets of brothers: James and John, sons of Zebedee; Simon and Andrew, sons of Jonas; and Matthew and James, sons of Alphaeus. James and John are cousins of Jesus; their mother, Salome, is a sister of Mary, the mother of Jesus.

4. As ludicrous as it seems, one of those chosen, Matthew, also known as Levi, is a tax collector —a vassal of Rome.

Interestingly, it seems likely that Matthew's brother James, who as I have said is also one of the twelve, is a Zealot. This must lead to some interesting family arguments.

Whether or not James is a Zealot, we know that at least one of the disciples, Simon, most certainly is! Indeed, he's known as Simon the Zealot. Everyone knows that the Zealots are out to overthrow the occupation by fair means or foul. Can you imagine the atmosphere between Matthew, a servant of Herod Antipas and the Romans, and Simon, a fanatical Jewish nationalist. What could possibly have been in the mind of the Nazarene? The choice of just these two will spell disaster for the movement.

But there's more!

5. Some of the disciples appear to have far from ideal temperaments for the job. Two examples will suffice to make the point. James and John, the sons of Zebedee, are popularly known as the sons of thunder —for obvious reasons. They are quick–tempered, insensitive, ambitious.

6. Not all the disciples are sold on the mission of Jesus. At least one of them, Judas Iscariot, is less than happy about the way things are turning out. "Teaching and miracles are alright in their place, but where's the earthly kingdom?" is what he is rumoured to be saying.

He's not alone in being less than 100% behind Jesus. One of the other disciples, Thomas, is quickly getting the nickname doubting Thomas. It seems that his first reaction is always not to believe what he is being asked to believe. How is Jesus ever going to win over the general populace when his disciples are not completely convinced, and different factions are pulling in opposite directions?

I anticipate and I predict disaster! There is no way that this motley band can help this man to succeed. For the record, and as a convenient case study for future teaching purposes, I shall monitor the situation closely. The thirteen are being carried along at the moment by the charisma of the leader and the miracles of healing that are making him extremely popular. But will it last?

It did not, of course, and the next entry in the file is headed *Mission Failure*. It follows soon after the untimely death of Jesus by crucifixion. It has the obvious 'told you so' message. I quote:

As we anticipated, the Jesus campaign has floundered. It seems that the one Judean in the band, Judas Iscariot, betrayed him, for a mere thirty pieces of silver, and then committed suicide.

Apart, possibly, from John, the rest of the disciples deserted him at his hour of greatest need. Peter, the rustic, loud–mouthed Galilean fisherman, is known to have denied three times that he even knew Jesus.

We learn that John has agreed to look after the mother of Jesus, but the whereabouts of most of the others is unknown. If only he had taken our advice —but given his uncompromising message and his choice of friends, his mission was doomed from the start.

There seems little point in following the case any further, but we will keep the file open, just in case there are unexpected developments.

Of course, with the benefit of hindsight, we know that the matter did not come to an abrupt end. There is a belated last entry in the file which has a decidedly upbeat message. It is headed, *"Where are they now? We got it wrong!"* It was written some decades after the death of Jesus, and acknowledges that there were several surprises and many unexpected happenings.

The cause of Jesus of Nazareth did not come to an abrupt end at the crucifixion. Many people now believe that he rose from the dead and this must have fired up his followers to spread the message. Yes, the *SAME DISCIPLES* we had criticised in earlier minutes —except Judas Iscariot, of course.

We can only assume that something must have happened to change them. They themselves put it down to encounters with the Holy Spirit, starting at the Feast of Pentecost soon after the crucifixion, but not limited to that initial event.

We can only believe that the change in them was superhuman, supernatural, especially in view of their success. You may have heard that they now have this reputation – "They have turned the world upside down!" Hard to believe, unless we invoke the God factor! Here is an update:

1. You will recall mention of James, the brother of John; he was one of the inner band of three who were closest to Jesus when he was alive. Well, James did not last long. He was killed by Herod, by the sword, apparently to teach the new movement a lesson.

2. James' brother, John, has been exiled to the isle of Patmos, where he continues to write. Interestingly, he is now known as the apostle of love —a long way from the name 'son of thunder', by which he was known in his early days.

3. Very soon after that Feast of Pentecost, Peter became the clear leader of the group, showing incredible courage and daring – quite a change from the weakling who denied that he even knew Jesus. The word is out that Peter has been crucified in Rome —but only after nearly thirty years of faithful service. He was crucified head down—at his own

request, believing that he was not worthy to die as his Lord had died.

4. It seems that Simon Peter's brother, Andrew, has also died as a martyr, probably in the town of Patras in Greece. Like his brother, he felt unworthy to die as his Lord had died. In his case he was crucified on an X–shaped cross.

5. The amazing story goes on. It is widely believed that 'doubting Thomas' went as far as India with the message of Jesus. The word is that he has also died as a martyr.

6. Matthew, the former tax collector, could certainly use a pen, of course, and news is out that he has written a 'life of Jesus'.

And so it goes on. Time will not permit us to expand on the exploits of the rest of the original disciples. Sufficient to say that Philip went east to preach in Asia, before coming to a martyr's end. Simon the Zealot was also still there, ready to go on serving Jesus following the crucifixion, having put away the dagger. Where did he go? Some say to Egypt, others to Persia, but no-one really knows for certain. It is generally believed that he, too, was a martyr, along with someone called Jude.

This is an amazing story by any standard, and one that surely cannot be explained without invoking the God factor. Indeed, I have no quibbles with the earlier entries in the Jesus file —they are based on sound logic. The only thing they did not allow for was the divine!

So ends the Jesus file. It survived betrayal. It survived

denial. It survived the doubts of a Thomas. It survived the potential time bomb in the contact between Matthew the tax collector and Simon the Zealot. It survived the fact that most of the disciples were basically uneducated and common. It survived —to turn the world upside down!

And let us never underestimate the changes that took place amongst the eleven. A 'son of thunder' like John becomes an apostle of love. A weakling like Peter becomes a courageous church leader. A relative outsider, like Andrew, can be content to remain in the shadow of his brother, Peter, and act with graciousness, being prepared to take second place. A tax collector and a Zealot can miraculously live together in harmony. Little wonder that the world was turned upside down.

EXPLANATION

Some verses from the Acts of the Apostles:

> Then they [the disciples] returned to Jerusalem from the hill called the Mount of Olives, a Sabbath day's walk from the city. When they arrived, they went upstairs to the room where they were staying. Those present were Peter, John, James and Andrew; Philip and Thomas, Bartholomew and Matthew; James son of Alphaeus and Simon the Zealot, and Judas son of James. They all joined together constantly in prayer....[1]
>
> When the day of Pentecost came, they were all together in one place. Suddenly a sound like the

blowing of a violent wind came from heaven and filled the whole house where they were sitting. They saw what seemed to be tongues of fire that separated and came to rest on each of them.   All of them were filled with the Holy Spirit and began to speak in other tongues as the Spirit enabled them....[2]

Then Peter stood up with the Eleven, raised his voice and addressed the crowd....[3]

4

Someone in the Jerusalem Crowd

"You disowned the Holy and Righteous One and
asked that a murderer be released to you. You killed
the author of life, but God raised him from the
dead."[1]

Poignant words by any standards, but in my case they
were life changing. They made me take stock, reminding
me of my original choice; but they allowed me to choose
again. What a choice! —Jesus Barabbas or Jesus of
Nazareth who is also called Christ. We disowned the Holy
and Righteous One and had asked instead for the release
of a murderer.

Here were two plebeian fishermen from Galilee, who
were taking on the whole of the religious establishment
and trying to convince the rest of us at the same time, but
more of that in a moment. Let me go back a little and say
something about my original choice. It all centres around

the one who is called Jesus of Nazareth. He had the reputation of being a miracle worker, and was known as an incisive teacher. For a while he had the people with him and was extremely popular. The common people saw him as an answer to a long standing prayer for a Messiah —to rid us of Roman domination, amongst other things. But he seemed to draw back; his mission was somewhere else or something else, and disillusionment set in. But the high priests and the other religious leaders saw him as a threat, and you had there all the ingredients of a disaster.

Human nature being what it is, hopes were raised when, a few weeks ago, he rode into Jerusalem in triumph, and many of us were happy to cry out, "Hosanna to the Son of David; Blessed is He who comes in the name of the Lord." That was some day! Perhaps he was the answer after all: the long expected Messiah! But just as quickly, the euphoria evaporated, and within a few days he was captured by our leaders and exposed to a hastily arranged trial. It was Passover time; it was all so frenetic and, in retrospect, completely contrived. Our leaders were accusing him of everything, including blasphemy and sedition. This was only a few days after that triumphant entry into Jerusalem, but he was now before the Roman procurator, Pilate, on trial for his life.

Any casual observer could see that Pilate was convinced that Jesus was innocent, but he did not seem to want to offend our leaders. He would duck and weave, but they kept coming after him. He tried everything; he even sent Jesus to King Herod, who was hardly a friend of his at the time. But it was all to no avail. In some ways I felt sorry for Pilate, but in another sense I thought it was all so pathetic. At the time, I was fairly indifferent, but there I was in front of the Roman Praetorium early one morning—a part of a general crowd. Many of us were there out of curiosity.

I cannot say I was too impressed by Jesus at the time. He did not seem to be doing his case any good. There was no ducking or weaving on his part; he would come out with answers that were guaranteed to infuriate our leaders and at the same time to frustrate the Romans.

Nor was I too impressed by his followers. They were conspicuous by their absence. He was very much on his own. I could not help feeling that they were a pathetic bunch. They were certainly no advertisement for his teaching or charisma, having voted with their feet!

Then there was the event that I referred to at the beginning. Maybe you need some of the background. The basic point revolves around a tradition that had been instituted by the Romans themselves. At Passover time, it was their custom to release to us a prisoner of our choosing. Of course, Passover reminded us of our release from slavery in Egypt, and that was probably the motive behind the gesture. You could argue that setting convicted prisoners free was hardly guaranteed to improve law and order in the land, but then the choice was left to us, so little harm was normally done.

I do not know the full story, and my memory is rather vague as to what actually happened. Some of my friends who were there seemed to feel that the initiative came from us. I do not think so, somehow. It seemed to me to be a last gasp effort on the part of Pilate to release this man Jesus, without causing a damaging riot. Let me explain.

As a matter of tactics on this occasion, Pilate did not give us a free choice. Essentially, he presented us with an ultimatum. He was going to release either Jesus or a notorious criminal called Barabbas. That was the choice before us! Now I need to tell you something about this Barabbas before I explain what I believe Pilate had in the back of his mind. I seem to recall that the fellow was actually called Jesus Barabbas, so we had to choose between Jesus Barabbas or Jesus who was also called Christ. Now this Barabbas was guilty of at least three crimes: (i) He was a thief and a robber. (ii) He was a murderer, and (iii) he had taken part in an insurrection against the Romans. He was undoubtedly one of the ringleaders. In our language, Barabbas means *son of his father*. I suppose you might say he was 'his father's son'. This may have been a name of endearment, but somehow I do not think so. He was what I would call a lewd fellow of the baser sort. Hardly someone you would want to introduce to your daughter. So Pilate gave us an intriguing choice: Barabbas or Jesus. What was his motive? It is hard to decide, but let me hazard a few guesses.

In the first place, Pilate may have thought that Jesus was popular with our common people. So a conciliatory gesture to the populace, and perhaps a snub to the priests, was in his mind. He obviously knew of the hatred of our religious leaders, but had heard about the triumphal entry into Jerusalem, so perhaps he was counting on the goodwill of the general populace. He may also have felt that Barabbas was such a vile person that no self–respecting Jew would vote for his release. How wrong he was! Pilate may also have been shrewder than we give him credit for. Do not forget that one of the planks of our leaders' case against Jesus was that he was guilty of sedition. What was it they said? "He stirs up the people! He is a bothersome agitator. He is guilty of sedition!" So Pilate may have reasoned this way: the high priests can hardly ask for the release of someone who has already been found guilty of the same crime of sedition. It is intriguing.

So, was it a last ditch effort on the part of Pilate? Or was he quietly confident that he had finally found an *out*? I do not know, but what I do know is that he misjudged us and our leaders. Barabbas may have been a vile fellow, a thief and a murderer, but he was also a freedom fighter, a Zealot, ostensibly attempting to rid us of Roman domination. For some, this counted for a lot!

Then there were the wily chief priests. They did not need to get their hands dirty themselves; neither did they need to compromise their case against Jesus. All they needed to do was to quietly incite the rest of us —and this they did very successfully. They knew enough about group dynamics; they knew how easily a spontaneous popular demonstration can be staged. Yes, they knew enough about human nature, and we fell for it! To a man, we fell for it! We were like a flock of sheep.

"Away with this man! Release Barabbas to us." Of Jesus, we shouted: "Crucify him!" Yes, the Galilean preacher was right —we chose Barabbas that day, rather than Jesus. We chose a murderer rather than Jesus!

Looking back, it is clear that our leaders were much more concerned about getting their man than about releasing Barabbas. At the time, it was a diversion, an irritant. The chief priests were not at all concerned about the wellbeing of Barabbas —how could they be? For the rest of us, our motives were mixed; there was some hatred, yes; some frustration, definitely; but basically there was a general indifference and ignorance, and there was, all the time, the 'herd instinct'. I do not think I am being untruthful. I had no big axe to grind. I did not feel too much hatred for the fellow, but I was happy to go along with it. There was certainly guilt by association. Maybe there's a bit of the nationalist in me. I did not then understand the real reason why he was to die. I was certainly incensed by his cowardly followers. And, after all, if our religious leaders felt that he deserved to die, who was I to object? But the truth is that I do not know why I cast my vote as a yes! My family were waving palms one day, and less than a week later I was voting for his death and the release of a criminal. The preacher was right. Some of our people walked away at that point, not wanting to be associated with the hypocrisy. They felt that by so doing they were appeasing their consciences, but they were as guilty as the rest of us. The preacher was right. We disowned the Holy and Righteous one and asked that a murderer be released to us.

But it is all water under the bridge now although, for many, it left its mark. You will know that what followed was somewhat eerie? We had our way of course. Jesus of Nazareth was crucified —between two thieves in fact, who may have been friends of Barabbas. The middle cross was undoubtedly marked out for Barabbas. He was now free and Jesus was there in his place.

We had been crying out for blood, but I have to tell you that when it came there was no euphoria, no sense of elation, only a massive anticlimax —even the weather reflected our mood. Was it all worth it? Had we done the right thing? We consoled ourselves with the knowledge that our religious leaders were happy, and that his own followers were good for nothing cowards. But I vividly recall the quietness, the darkness at the height of the day.

There was no further time for melancholy and

contemplation. It was Passover. That was the biggest feast of the year for us, commemorating our release from the slavery of Egypt. At this feast we would get hold of an unblemished male lamb and have it carefully killed and prepared. We would meet as families at sundown, sing some psalms, drink some wine and have a meal together. The Passover did not give us much time for contemplation, but then the rumours began to spread! —incredible tales about Jesus of Nazareth rising from the dead. It all seemed too far–fetched at the time. I had seen him on the cross, and he was dead alright! People do not rise from the dead, I convinced myself. But the general mood was certainly changing.

Our religious leaders were getting jittery, the rumours were gaining in momentum, but I remained sceptical. Then, at another of our feasts, fifty days or so later, things really did begin to happen; incredible events with some bizarre behaviour. People were talking with conviction in different languages, and taking us to task for what had happened. They were insisting that Jesus of Nazareth was the Lord, the Christ, in fact the Son of the Living God.

I was not sure whether to take things seriously, but I will tell you what impressed me. His pathetic band of followers were now in the vanguard! Yes, that same group of disciples, who had seemed so downhearted, were now leading the way. From what I gather, the preachers were quoting from our Scriptures, saying that the crucifixion was a part of some divine strategy, that we *all* acted in ignorance, even our leaders, and that there was an out —if we were willing to repent.

Anyway, judging from the response, many people were convinced. I have heard a figure of three thousand mentioned.

For me there was plenty of food for thought, but the authorities were still on the warpath and I was prepared to see how things developed. I suppose that reflected my conservative and sceptical nature. But I was becoming suspicious of the fickleness of our attitude to this man. One day we were shouting "Hosanna", then it was "Crucify him." Now the very same people were praising God for him again.

Anyway, one afternoon the most amazing thing happened before my very eyes. I happened to be near a gate of the temple that was called 'Beautiful', a place where it is customary for beggars to sit. It was about three o'clock, when our people would be expected to be at prayer. At the trial I had heard a fellow with a Galilean accent deny that he knew Jesus. He was quite firm on the point, becoming rather angry. Well this same fellow, together with a friend, were now helping a crippled man to his feet, saying that they were doing it in the name of Jesus. The man was a well known beggar, in his forties; he had been a cripple from birth. Was this really the cripple I had seen sitting in that place for as long as I can remember? Yes! And the Galilean? Was this the same pathetic fellow who had warmed his hands by the fire at the trial and had perjured himself? Apparently, yes. But now he seemed to have a charisma, an inner confidence and an indefinable power. The miracle did his cause no harm at all, of course, and I was now ready to listen to him. We were in Solomon's Porch by this time.

And there it was again. I heard Peter speaking of Jesus, words that really struck home:

"You handed him over to be killed, and you disowned him before Pilate, though he had decided to let him go. You disowned the Holy and Righteous One and asked that a murderer be released to you. You killed the author of life, but God raised him from the dead. We are witnesses of this. By faith in the name of Jesus this man whom you see and know was made strong. It is Jesus' name and the faith that comes through him that has given this complete healing to him, as you can all see.

Now, brothers, I know that you acted in ignorance, as did your leaders...."[2]

So there it was: a crippled man healed, cowardly disciples now preaching with a supernatural power, and an inner voice saying it must somehow be true. I remember saying, "Oh God, forgive me —but what does it all mean? How do I square it up with what I've always been taught about crucifixion?" I had learnt long before that there was a curse on anyone who had been crucified, and here I was, with a need to acknowledge that a crucified prophet had been raised from the dead and was indeed the author of life. I thought hard and long, and sought advice from some of the new believers nearby. Suddenly it all fell into place. The answer was staring me in the face. It was all over our Scriptures, from as far back as the story of Abraham and Isaac, when God provided a sacrifice. It was certainly in the imagery of the Passover feast, which we had so recently celebrated. Take an unblemished lamb and sacrifice it. And what was it we were saying at the feast? "The stone the builders rejected has become the capstone; the LORD has done this, and it is marvellous in our eyes."[3] The psalmist must surely have been pointing ahead to Jesus as he penned those words. But it was a reading from the prophecy of Isaiah that finally clinched it for me.

Who has believed our message and to whom has the arm of the LORD been revealed? He grew up before him like a tender shoot, and like a root out of dry ground. He had no beauty or majesty to attract us to him, nothing in his appearance that we should desire him. He was despised and rejected by men, a man of sorrows, and familiar with suffering. Like one from whom men hide their faces he was despised, and we esteemed him not. Surely he took up our infirmities and carried our sorrows, yet we considered him stricken by God, smitten by him, and afflicted. But he was pierced for our transgressions, he was crushed for our iniquities; the punishment that brought us peace was upon him, and by his wounds we are healed. We all, like sheep, have gone astray, each of us has turned to his own way; and the LORD has laid on him the iniquity of us all.[4]

In my place, condemned he stood; he had sealed my pardon with his blood. It was not only Barabbas who could say: I should have been on that cross. Jesus was there in *my* place, also.

As to the matter of the curse on anyone hung on a cross, I was shown the meaning of that as well. It was explained to me that Jesus took on himself the curses that had resulted from our disobedience to the law of God. Part of what Jesus won for me on the cross was release from a curse.[5]

So, I wondered, where do I go from here? Peter, and his friend John, left me in no doubt. I had to repent; I had to believe; and then I had to get baptized. Repentance essentially meant both saying sorry and turning away from all that had separated me from God; and, if I was really guilty by association of nailing Jesus to the cross, repentance was not difficult. I had to believe. I had seen enough: Peter and John changed; a cripple healed; others changed beyond recognition; the Scriptures affirming what had happened. I was happy to acknowledge that Jesus of Nazareth had been raised from the dead; that he was the Lamb of God, who had died for me, that I might live. He, Jesus, was the author of life. I now needed to make my commitment public and to be identified with the followers of Jesus. The disciples explained these things to me, and that times of refreshing would come from the Lord. I would know the same Holy Spirit, whose power the disciples of Jesus had experienced on the great day of the Feast. And I was not alone. I was just one of about five thousand who responded to the Lord.

5

Gamaliel

It is now fifteen years since the death and resurrection of Jesus Christ and the formation of the fledgling church in Jerusalem, following the outpouring of the Holy Spirit on that amazing Day of Pentecost. You will know that we have seen significant growth during that time, and the church has now spread its wings into Gentile territory.

This may, therefore, be a good time for us to put into perspective the major events and influences that have helped to shape our present church structures. Each member of the church leadership has been given specific tasks in this exercise, and one of mine has been to assess the influence of Gamaliel in shaping the church of the early days. It has not been easy, since the many soundings I have taken from those who had first hand experiences of the relevant events have not left me with a strong consensus either way. Some have been quite complimentary and have spoken highly of Gamaliel, while others have been equivocal, to say the least. I will allow you to judge for yourself, after I have laid out the strengths and weaknesses of the man, and have reminded you of his role in the days either side of the resurrection of Jesus.

Gamaliel is a Pharisee, a teacher of the Law, and it is probably true to say that he is respected by the vast majority of the people. He is a so-called Rabban, one of the highest honours of the Jewish faith, equivalent, I suppose, to one of your professors of theology. He has had a number of outstanding students. Interestingly, the most illustrious has been one called Saul of Tarsus, someone who was thrust so dramatically into the limelight. You must know of Saul, that fiery persecutor of our church, until he was dramatically apprehended by Jesus on his way to Damascus. We now know him as Paul, the apostle to the Gentiles.

But, given the task I was set, I felt I needed to give serious consideration to those early days when Saul sat at the feet of Gamaliel, soaking up all the wealth of experience and wisdom. Certainly, we are at liberty to question whether Saul's persecution of the church was simply an outworking of some of Gamaliel's teaching. We do not know for sure. We have not questioned Saul on the matter. Perhaps he came to his own conclusions; perhaps he could see that this new movement of ours contained within it something that could destroy the very edifice of the Jewish faith. What I do know is that in one rabbinic document to which I have had access, there is a statement which might throw some light on things. It says, 'The great Rabbi Gamaliel has had amongst his disciples one who gave his master a good deal of trouble, manifesting impudence in matters of learning.' I wonder whether this could be referring to Saul. If it does, we can excuse

Gamaliel from many of Saul's excesses in his pre-conversion days! However, let us now address the impact Gamaliel had on the events surrounding the death and resurrection of Jesus.

We need to remind ourselves that the Sanhedrin, of which Gamaliel was a respected member, had seen to it that Jesus was found guilty of a capital offence. He was crucified between two thieves, and his body was then placed in a tomb. So far as the Sanhedrin was concerned, that was that. But as we are only too eager to tell everyone, that was not that! Three days after the crucifixion, the tomb was found empty; his once pathetic band of followers, of which I was one, was now fired up with a confident belief that Jesus had been raised from the dead. We went into the streets of Jerusalem, telling everyone about the resurrection, proclaiming that everybody, including members of the Sanhedrin, should repent and turn to Christ. Not surprisingly, members of the Sanhedrin were not amused, and both the Pharisees and the Sadducees on the ruling body decided to stamp out these astonishing stories once and for all. It turned out that this was not as simple as all that, since the disciples seemed to have supernatural powers to heal, and an amazing miracle, involving a blind beggar, took place near the temple in Jerusalem. The inevitable head-to-head confrontation resulted in the two disciples involved, Peter and John, being hauled before the Sanhedrin. Remarkably, Peter, who a little earlier (at the time of the crucifixion) had been known for his cowardice, was now telling the Pharisees and the Sadducees on the Council that he had to obey God rather than them! Not unnaturally, the Pharisees, and especially the Sadducees, were having none of this, and in their fury they would have had Peter and John put to death there and then. It was at this point that Gamaliel took centre stage. He first had Peter and John taken outside the courtroom, before he addressed the Sanhedrin. In many ways, his advice was standard rabbinical teaching, and certainly not peculiar to Gamaliel; but he used it to good effect.

"Men of Israel, consider carefully what you intend to do to these men. Some time ago Theudas appeared, claiming to be somebody, and about four hundred men rallied to him. He was killed, all his followers were dispersed, and it all came to nothing. After him, Judas the Galilean appeared in the days of the census and led a band of people in revolt. He too was killed, and all his followers were scattered. Therefore, in the present case I advise you: Leave these men alone! Let them go! For if their purpose or activity is of human origin, it will fail. But if it is from God, you will not be able to stop these men; you will only find yourselves fighting against God."[1]

Although this is not the place to debate the validity or otherwise of this rabbinic teaching, it is important for me to digress a little at this point to stress one immediate consequence of what Gamaliel was saying. As a highly respected member of the Council, he was admitting the possibility that our movement might be of God. By implication, the Sanhedrin could have had no conclusive proof, no proof at all, that the claims that Jesus Christ had risen from the dead were not true. Their antagonism was seemingly based not on reason or fact, but on baser motives. I believe this point cannot be overstressed!

However, back to the events at the meeting of the Sanhedrin. So persuasive were Gamaliel's arguments that, to a man, the Sanhedrin voted *not* to put the disciples to death. Instead, they had Peter and John flogged and, with a further pat on the wrists, they were told not to do it again.

The response of the disciples is now well known. They left the Sanhedrin *rejoicing* because they had been counted worthy to suffer disgrace for Jesus' sake, and *they continued to proclaim the good news that Jesus was the Christ.*

So, that is the background to the major impact that Gamaliel had on the early developments in our Jerusalem church. In one sense, there was Gamaliel, a pillar of society, deeply religious, intelligent, wise, and an unexpected ally of the disciples, possibly saving our young church from annihilation. Some would say that these are impressive credentials by any standards. However, I have yet to address the most important issue. What was Gamaliel's attitude to our Lord and Master? Clearly, he was no enemy as I have attempted to show, and his timely interjection did save Peter and John from death. Indirectly, therefore, our young church could be seen to be in his debt. Nonetheless, it is my considered judgment that, if the Sanhedrin had done away with Peter and John, our fledgling church would *not* have died. I know that Peter and John were quietly thankful for Gamaliel's interjection —who would not have been? But it is my strong conviction that persecution will always be a *positive* influence on the spread of the gospel. I am sure that as the story of the church unfolds in the coming days, there will be ample evidence to prove that what I am saying is correct. In a nutshell, the fact is that the blood of martyrs will be the seed of the church. I can already point to the martyrdom of Stephen, 'one of the seven', as a recent proof of my assertion.

So we need to look elsewhere for a substantive reason to commend the impact of Gamaliel on the spread of the gospel. You see, there is a big downside. Let us never forget that Gamaliel kept his seat on the Sanhedrin all through the arrest of Jesus, through the trial and through the crucifixion. I submit, therefore, that he was guilty, at least by association, of the death of our Lord and Master. He may be a pillar of Jewish society, but he was no friend to Jesus. Later, his advice to the Sanhedrin averted serious trouble and death perhaps, but Peter and John were still flogged for their troubles! And what, I ask, was Gamaliel's fundamental motive? It is unlikely that he supported the basic message of the disciples, so although he may have saved the lives of Peter and John, his real desire was probably to prevent a division in the Council and, at the same time, to avoid aggravating the Romans. I submit that he was all for toleration; he was an opportunist, a politician. There is no evidence that I know of that would suggest that Gamaliel has embraced our faith.

In contrast, I would ask you to look at Peter and John, regarded as unlearned and ignorant men by members of the Sanhedrin, but more than a match for them nevertheless. Fishermen they may once have been, with strong, grating, Galilean accents, but our Lord had touched their lives and, following the resurrection and the outpouring of the Holy Spirit at Pentecost, they were dramatically filled with supernatural courage and dynamic power. This is the church I represent; not with a polite, non-committal stance on eternal issues, but with a firm conviction that Jesus has been made both Lord and Christ.

What was it the Sanhedrin said to Peter and John on that momentous day? "We gave you strict orders not to teach in this name. Yet, you have filled Jerusalem with your teaching...." Did flogging bring an end to it all? By no means, since day after day in the temple courts, and from house to house, the disciples never stopped proclaiming the good news that Jesus is the Christ.

This is a true picture of the church: unstoppable, invincible, with an all-consuming passion for Jesus Christ. Where does Gamaliel fit into this scheme of things? His wisdom, learning, piety and reputation may have been impressive, but we still longed for him to come down off the fence.

So my report on Gamaliel, of necessity, will have to be a negative one.

AN UPDATE

About a hundred years ago, there was a Scottish preacher by the name of Alexander Whyte. He had an influential ministry, in a church known as Free St. George's. In one of his Sunday communion addresses, he took Gamaliel as his subject and came to a rather negative conclusion about him. Summing up, he turned his attention to the young men in the congregation and said, in the language of his day: "Young men, with your life still before you, Gamaliel, the fluent and applauded opportunist, is here written with a special eye to your learning. Make your choice! It is an awful thing to say, but it is the simple truth. God and his Son, his church and his gospel, all stand before your door at this moment, waiting for your choice and your decision. Gamaliel decided, and his day is past, and he is in his own place. And now is your day of decision. Make up your minds. Take the step! Take sides with Peter and John. Take sides with Jesus Christ! And that step will solve for you a thousand perplexities and will deliver you from a thousand snares. You will be the children of the light and of the day and you will walk in the light, when other men all around you are stumbling in darkness. Suppose that you had been Gamaliel and act now, as you so clearly see how he should have acted then."

6

John Mark

I was brought up in Jerusalem. We were fairly wealthy. Mary, my mother, was a widow, and she had a large house.

The events of the crucifixion are still vivid in my memory. I was rather young at the time, and inquisitive, so much so that on the terrible night when Jesus was betrayed, arrested and tried, I ventured out into the streets of Jerusalem alone —covered only by a linen garment. I followed Jesus—at a distance—but I was discovered. I became gripped with fear, the linen garment fell to the ground, and I ran off naked from the scene. You do not quickly forget events like that!

During the earthly ministry of Jesus, and also following his resurrection, my home was used as a meeting place, so I got to know the disciples. In fact, I became a Christian through the ministry of the apostle Peter, and as a result he saw me very much as his son in the faith.

Talking of Peter, you may have heard of that famous incident when he escaped miraculously from prison. It was at a time of particular tension and opposition for the young church. James the apostle had been killed by Herod Agrippa, and Peter was imprisoned, awaiting a similar fate. His trial was delayed because of the Passover feast. However, that trial never did take place. Amazingly, Peter found himself OUTSIDE the prison, without a soldier in sight. Where do you think he headed? To my home, where many Christians were meeting for prayer. It was late, but we were earnestly praying for Peter's release — praying with much fervour, but only a little faith. You have probably heard of the difficulty Peter had in getting into my home? Rhoda, our servant girl, heard him knocking at the outer door. She recognized Peter's voice, but in her excitement she forgot to open the door! Instead, she ran to the assembled throng with the amazing news. Do you think they believed her? Not a bit of it! There they were, earnestly praying for Peter's release, with little, if any, expectation of a positive response from the Lord. It worked out alright of course. Those were exciting days at my home —but enough of this rambling.

Joseph, a cousin of mine on my mother's side, will play a prominent role in our unfolding story. He hails from Cyprus. He is a Jew, of course, like me; in fact, he is a Levite, coming from the priestly tribe of our nation. Like my mother, Joseph was also reasonably rich and he owned a good slice of land. Those of you who know the Scriptures well may find this strange. In the old days, the Levites were not allowed to own *any* property; they were expected to live off the tithes of the rest of the Jews. But over the years things changed greatly, and now Levites are often quite wealthy, and they can certainly own land. I stress this point because it was land ownership which first brought Joseph to the attention of the infant church.

I do not know when precisely he became a follower of Jesus, but what I do know is that during those heady days when the church members were sharing everything, Joseph sold some of his land and laid it at the feet of the apostles. Now, Joseph was and is in every way a *good* man, with many admirable qualities that I greatly admire. He is a man of noble stature; wherever he goes he has a genius for lifting the mood *and* the spirit of the people; he has a gift for encouraging them. Immediately, the leaders of the church recognized him as being full of the Holy Spirit and faith. So impressed were they, that they gave him another name —Barnabas, or 'son of consolation', 'son of encouragement'. And the name stuck, so even we, his kinsfolk, now call him Barnabas, not Joseph.

Looking back, I can see how cousin Barnabas played a pivotal role in the early expansion of the church, although he has since been somewhat eclipsed by Peter and, especially, Paul.

Talking of Paul (or Saul, as he once was), you probably know that Barnabas was a great help to him in his early years as a Christian. I am thinking of when Saul returned to Jerusalem for the first time since his conversion, only to be feared and shunned by the Christians there. When they had last seen him, a year or so earlier, he was breathing out murderous threats against the church. Little wonder that the disciples were afraid when he returned; some of them just could not bring themselves to believe that he was now a Christian. But Barnabas came to Saul's rescue. He staked his good name on the man, explaining how Saul had been soundly converted on his way to Damascus. So convincing was Barnabas that Saul was accepted by the Christians; he was allowed to move freely about Jerusalem to preach the gospel. It was only when he ran into trouble with some Grecian Jews, who wanted to kill him, that the church leaders decided that he should return to Tarsus, his home town. The point I want to make is that Saul might have failed and fallen foul of the church if it had not been for the encouragement and support of Barnabas. By these actions, my cousin built up an impressive reputation, especially amongst the leaders of the Jerusalem church.

You will be aware that, in the early days, the church in Jerusalem was regarded as having some seniority, for obvious reasons. Then, slowly but surely, it was eclipsed by the church at Antioch, which is over four hundred kilometres to the north, in the province of Syria. Antioch is a large city, with over half a million inhabitants. Though predominantly Greek, it also has a sizeable Jewish colony.

The inevitable shift to Antioch followed the persecution of the Jerusalem Christians, which took place after the martyrdom of Stephen. The Christians were scattered in every direction, including Antioch, and in this way the gospel spread. In the early days, the impact was felt by the Jews only, but some Christians came over from Cyprus and Cyrene and they began a very important work amongst the Gentiles as well. In fact, many people, both Jews and Gentiles, were converted in Antioch at that time, and a strong and vibrant church was formed there.

You will not be surprised to learn that the Jerusalem church was intrigued by these developments, as well as encouraged —so they decided to send someone to Antioch to investigate. And do you know who they sent? Yes, cousin Barnabas. When he arrived in Antioch, he was thrilled by what he saw. There was patently a significant move of God's Spirit amongst the Jews and the Gentiles. But Barnabas quickly realized that the responsibility laid on him by Jerusalem was too much for one man. He did not know of anyone from Jerusalem suitable to help him, but he did recall the potential of Saul of Tarsus. You need to know that by this time, Saul had been a Christian for almost ten years. He had spent much of that time preaching in the area around Tarsus, when he was not earning his living as a tentmaker. (Incidentally, Barnabas also feels strongly that he should not be a financial burden on the church, and he earns his own living as well.)

Without reference to Jerusalem, Barnabas went the hundred and eighty kilometres to Tarsus to seek out Saul. It was on his own initiative. I can only assume that Saul was eager to get more involved in the Lord's work and, when he and Barnabas returned to Antioch, a close association and friendship, which would last for almost ten years, was cemented. The early years were spent in Antioch.

It was around this time that the followers of Jesus in Antioch were first called 'Christians' —people of Christ. This was originally a term of contempt, coined by those who were certainly not sympathetic to the gospel message, but, as you know, the name has stuck.

Let me pick out one event of interest from the Antioch experience. Agabus, a prophet from the Jerusalem church, predicted that a severe famine would arise over quite a wide area. The church at Antioch decided that Jerusalem was likely to be worse hit than themselves, so they decided to send practical financial help to the Jerusalem Christians —and this they did through Barnabas and Saul. Remember that this meant a journey of over 400 kms.

While in Jerusalem, there were some exciting

developments, but also troubling events, like the martyrdom of James which I have already mentioned. Anyway, on completion of their mission, Barnabas and Saul decided to return to Antioch and they invited me to join them, something I was more than happy to do, although I was still somewhat young, inexperienced, and maybe a little immature. Some of the leaders of the church in Antioch felt strongly that the time was right for Barnabas and Saul to set out on a major missionary enterprise, so we were commissioned by the church through the laying on of hands.

We all sailed for Paphos in Cyprus, where we witnessed some miracles and significant success for the gospel. The proconsul himself became a Christian. Cyprus was also notable for other less obvious signs of growth and change. It was there that Saul decided to forgo his Hebrew name and, from that time on, we knew him by his Greek name, Paul. This was also the time when Paul slowly but surely took centre stage and became the recognized leader of the group. Until this time the Christians spoke of Barnabas and Paul. After Cyprus, it was usually Paul and Barnabas.

From Cyprus we sailed to Perga in Pamphylia, and it was there that I decided to leave Paul and Barnabas. It would be an understatement to say that Paul was not amused! Why did I leave? Well, for a mixture of reasons, I suppose. But let me tell you what others have said on the matter. Some have hinted that I was unhappy that cousin Barnabas was essentially relegated to second place as the missionary enterprise progressed; not that I heard any complaints from my cousin, by the way. As I have said, there was a shortage of food in Jerusalem and I was naturally concerned about my mother's welfare. There may have been a touch of homesickness in the decision.

You also need to know that Paul and Barnabas were about to embark on a journey through very difficult terrain to the interior towns —and this was not a very attractive proposition! But whatever people may say, the fact remains that I absconded at this point and it took a long, long time for the matter to be resolved.

Anyway, after I left the group, things apparently progressed splendidly, and Paul and Barnabas had some thrilling experiences: miracles of healing, signs and wonders, clashes with the forces of Satan, yes; but all the time, and in every place they visited, Christians were encouraged and excited, and many new converts were added to the church. When they finally returned to Antioch, I understand that they called the whole church together and shared with them all that God had accomplished through them.

After the exertions of their missionary endeavours, Paul and Barnabas were to stay put in Antioch for a while. Not for the first time, they came across some bigoted Jewish Christians who could not let go of some of their Jewish roots and practices. They wanted all the Christians (Jews and Gentiles) to be circumcised and all that. So, off went Paul and Barnabas again to sort things out with the church in Jerusalem. Another four hundred kilometre trek! —which they did, of course, before the famous Council meeting, where James the brother of Jesus, and Peter, held forth. The upshot of the meeting was that Paul and Barnabas were given a letter which seemed to settle the matter once and for all, without inflicting too many conditions on the Gentile Christians. And on their return to Antioch, Paul and Barnabas again spent time encouraging the church and preaching the gospel, with a reasonable degree of peace and freedom, armed of course with the encouraging letter from the Jerusalem leaders. But all was not as it seemed, and there were the first signs of a rift between Paul and Barnabas. This is what happened. The apostle Peter visited Antioch and was happy to eat with the Gentile Christians, something he would never have done some years earlier. However, when James, the Lord's brother, also visited the city, Peter withdrew from eating with the Greeks —not to offend James, of course. It seems that cousin Barnabas, for all his earlier enthusiasm for the Gentile cause, had also been taken in. Paul was not amused and, to their faces, he confronted both Peter and Barnabas. I wonder when this running sore will be healed.

I believe that the contretemps between Paul and Barnabas was put right, but I was to be responsible for a much more serious disagreement between the two of them. After quite a long stay in Antioch, stretching for the best part of two years, for obvious reasons Paul wanted to return to the churches he had helped to found and establish on the first missionary enterprise. He wanted to see how they were progressing, and also to encourage them, of course. Quite naturally, he hoped that Barnabas would accompany him again. But Barnabas put to Paul the proposition that I should go with them. To say that Paul was opposed to that would be an understatement, and the suggestion led to a severe argument between those two great men. Neither would give in, and the rift between them became final. I regret that I was the cause of the break-up, but no compromise seemed possible. So Paul went off, accompanied by one of the Jerusalem leaders called Silas. They certainly had the backing and blessing of the Antioch leadership.

Barnabas dug his heels in and decided to go it alone with me in tow, so in one sense the church at Antioch had *two* missionary enterprises instead of one, but that is faint compensation, and it does not rectify the enormous damage that had been done to the Lord's work.

Speaking personally, I shall be forever grateful to my cousin for his faith in me at that time. I learnt much through his patience and encouragement. It was the first step in my rehabilitation. This became complete some time later when (I am glad to say) I was fully reconciled with Paul. I have helped him on several recent occasions, and here I am in Rome attending to his needs in his difficult prison situation. I have also interacted with Peter in recent years and, as you may know, I have recently completed a life of Jesus, a Gospel, which includes many of the experiences of Peter.

APPRAISAL

The period we have covered stretches from the death of Jesus to the imprisonment of Paul in Rome over thirty years later, although we have concentrated on one particular section of the story. It is a part which is full of signs and wonders, of opposition and victory, of battles within because of the Jew/Gentile problem, and battles without with the followers of Satan. It is, above all, a story of the work of the Holy Spirit taking place in and through Christians. It is full of instances of the supernatural hand of God over events. But what, especially, have the family members—Mary, Barnabas and John Mark—to teach us?

As far as we know, Mary was simply an 'enabler'. She

had a large house and she used it in the Lord's service. She was given to hospitality, and had what Paul calls 'the gift of helps'. Mary gave to the Lord what she had, and the Jerusalem Christians, especially Peter, had cause to thank God for her.

What of Barnabas? How the church needs men of his talents, Christians who will encourage us, console us, assist us, exhort us; men who will make goodness attractive.

I hear you ask: but what about the quarrel between Paul and Barnabas? This cannot be swept under the carpet! It is a salutary lesson that Paul and Barnabas, great as they were as Christian leaders, were not perfect. If we are looking for a perfect church, we shall be disappointed. If, at the first hint of dissension and murmurings, we are tempted to withdraw, it is good to remember that God's work survived the rift between Paul and Barnabas.

What of John Mark himself? His experiences would shout down the ages: **failure is not the end; restoration is possible!** Consider what Paul wrote as he neared the end of his ministry:

Only Luke is with me. Get Mark and bring him with you, because he is helpful to me in my ministry.[1]

7

Two of the Seven

I am writing from Caesarea on the Mediterranean coast, where I exercise a Christian ministry, ably assisted by my four daughters, who all have prophetic gifting. I have been here for close on twenty years and, although the ministry has been reasonably fruitful, it is a far cry from those remarkable days following the death and resurrection of Jesus, when I became deeply involved in the early expansion of the church.

I am known as Philip the evangelist! I am also known as 'one of the seven', a term I shall need to explain to you in some detail, before I bring you up to date with what I have been doing during the last twenty years or so. In the process, I shall need to introduce you to another of the original seven, by the name of Stephen. His life was cut short, very soon after we got together. This is the background.

In those exciting days following the birth of the church on that famous Day of Pentecost, the original disciples (minus Judas, and plus Matthias, of course) realized that there was only a limited amount of labour and ministry that they were capable of undertaking themselves. So they called together those of us men who comprised the church, and explained the situation. The solution was reasonably straightforward: the disciples would concentrate on prayer and ministry, and they asked us to choose seven men from amongst us to do the more mundane tasks. At the time, they lumped these jobs together under the interesting heading 'waiting on tables', although they in no way implied by this that they saw the work as unimportant and trivial. On the contrary.

The disciples laid down a set of parameters for the chosen seven, which were quite stringent. For example, we had to be men of good report, full of the Holy Spirit and wisdom! We were called 'deacons', and our major initial task was to sort out a problem associated with a group of Greek widows, who formed a part of the church at that time. There were rumblings that they were being discriminated against and were being neglected in the distribution of food —perhaps deliberately.

The seven of us who were chosen were all Greek–speaking Jews, so–called Hellenists, a shrewd choice in the circumstances! (Any student of human behaviour would see the logic of the choice. Nothing could so readily and quickly silence the murmurings.)

In addition to myself and Stephen there were Procurus, Nicanor, Timon, Parmenas and Nicholas, the latter being a Jewish convert who hailed from Antioch. It is true that the seven of us were chosen for practical work, but that did not constrain or limit us in any way, and Stephen and I in particular were encouraged to exercise a wider ministry as evangelists, preachers and teachers.

I cannot speak too highly of my fellow deacons, especially Stephen. He was certainly no Galilean peasant. He was bred a scholar, and he excelled in everything that was good and wholesome. He was a powerful apologist, and as a result it was difficult for his opponents to counter his arguments. Quite simply, he was full of special grace and power; and there was a disarming quality about him.

I have often wondered why Stephen, and myself for that matter, were thrust so suddenly into the limelight, almost ahead of the disciples. Maybe it was because the ruling body of the Jews, the Sanhedrin, was somewhat afraid of the disciples, and Stephen was someone they felt able to confront with venom. On the other hand, they may have despised Peter and John and the rest as unlearned and ignorant men and were perhaps glad to meet the intellectual challenge that Stephen provided. I do not really know the answer, but one thing is clear —Stephen was full of the power of God. He may not have convinced his adversaries, but he certainly confounded them. They resorted to force, and arrested him.

We still talk of Stephen's defence before the Sanhedrin! It contained a full history of the Jews, a virtual précis of God's dealing with them, drawing on the experiences of Abraham, Moses and the rest. But Stephen's uncompromising message that day fell on deaf ears: "You are just like your fathers: You always resist the Holy Spirit! Was there ever a prophet your fathers did not persecute? They even killed those who predicted the coming of the Righteous One. And now you have betrayed and murdered him."[1] He was talking of Jesus of Nazareth, of course. Those who heard Stephen speak attest that his face had been like that of an angel.

From that moment on, the events seemed to have a momentum of their own. Those who were there heard him say that he could see Jesus standing at the right hand of God! This was the last straw for the Jewish leaders. Yelling at the top of their voices, they dragged him out of the city and stoned him to death. To the very end, there was faith on Stephen's lips, when he prayed: "Lord Jesus, receive my spirit"; and forgiveness, too, as he fell to his knees and said, "Lord, do not hold this sin against them."

In my weaker moments, I have sometimes thought of Stephen's death, in human terms, as a tragic loss. He was so talented, but cut down in his prime. Could it have been avoided? What did it really accomplish? Could we see 'the hand of God' in it all? Without special pleading, we have come to the strong conclusion that the answer to the last question is in the affirmative!

You will have heard of someone called Saul of Tarsus. At that time, he was fanatically opposed to the church. Indeed, at the stoning of Stephen, he gave it his strong backing and even watched over the clothes of the assassins. But, however hard he tried, it seems that Saul never forgot that day and the way in which Stephen had died. In the short term, he dealt with this by even stronger opposition to our cause. But on one of his ferocious campaigns against us, everything changed dramatically. Saul met the risen Jesus on his way to Damascus. Saul of Tarsus was to become Paul the Apostle! The details of Saul's conversion must await another occasion, but we have the strong suspicion that we owe that conversion to the prayers and testimony of Stephen. That may be an over simplification, but there is no doubt in my mind that Paul was deeply influenced by the events that day, when Stephen was stoned to death. Is that special pleading? I do not think so, and there is something else that we feel we owe indirectly to Stephen's martyrdom. Jesus had told his disciples that he wanted them to be his witnesses, not only in Jerusalem, but also in Judea and Samaria and, indeed, to the outermost parts of the earth. You will know that the disciples found no difficulty fulfilling that command as far as Jerusalem was concerned, but there was certainly a reluctance to take the gospel message to Samaria. However, following Stephen's death, a great persecution broke out, and many members of the church were forced to scatter; but they made sure that they preached the gospel wherever they went! So, in a very real sense, the martyrdom of Stephen can be seen as having been instrumental in the taking the message of Jesus to the ends of the earth. Certainly, as I think of my dear departed fellow deacon, his death was not the unmitigated disaster it may have seemed at the time.

Interestingly, the persecution following Stephen's death seemed to bypass the disciples themselves, but I was one of those who was forced to leave Jerusalem by the persecution. I went down to Samaria, preaching the gospel as I went. You will no doubt have heard something about Samaria, if only to be able to quote: "the Jews have no dealings with the Samaritans." It is true, of course, and this state of affairs has existed for a millennium. Things got much worse about seven hundred years ago when Samaria was captured by the Assyrians, and many were deported. The country was re-populated by foreigners and, from that time, the Samaritans have been regarded as 'mongrels' by us Jews. To make matters worse, the Samaritans have a rival temple to ours; theirs is on Mount

Gerizim. To compound the matter, the only Scriptures they accept are the books of Moses, the so-called Pentateuch. Little wonder, then, that there is antipathy between the Jews and the Samaritans.

All this may explain why we were so reluctant to take seriously the command of Jesus to be his witnesses in Samaria! However, as I have indicated, a great persecution arose following the martyrdom of Stephen and, with the notable exception of the disciples, Christians were scattered throughout Judea and Samaria, and what you need to know is that the Christians preached as they went. It was in this way that the gospel spread throughout Samaria. I became involved at this point and, not to put a finer point on things, 'revival' broke out, many Samaritans became Christians, there were many miracles, and there was considerable joy throughout the region.

The disciples in Jerusalem got word of these amazing goings on, and they thought it prudent to send Peter and John to investigate. A distinctive part of their ministry at that time was to pray for the believers to receive the Holy Spirit, placing their hands on them. During these events, I assisted in a supportive role, leaving the initiatives and the major ministry to Peter and John.

At this time, there was a strange sequence of events, which defy rational explanation, although, for me, they were most decidedly prompted by God. Right at the heart of the revival in Samaria, when the gospel was making great strides amongst the local people, I felt an inner voice telling me quite specifically to leave there and to take the road south —the one that goes from Jerusalem to Gaza. The voice was telling me to go to the desert. You need to be very convinced of your actions before you undertake such a course! Try to imagine my situation at that time. In Samaria, there was great success, the whole area was stirred, masses of people were becoming Christians and great joy was evident everywhere. But I felt strangely constrained to travel into the desert for what turned out to be an interview with a lone traveller. From a teeming city to a lonely desert; from a place where I was ministering to a multitude, to a place where I had a congregation of one. The one happened to be a black diplomat from Ethiopia. He was obviously devout – in the Jewish sense. He was returning from a pilgrimage to Jerusalem and, when I met him, he was avidly reading the Scriptures, from Isaiah, as I recall.

I believe I need to tell you something about his home state and his role there. You see, it would be wrong to identify the Ethiopia I am talking about with the one you find in your present day atlases. When *we* talk of Ethiopia, we are referring to what would now be known as Northern Sudan; the Upper Nile, stretching from Aswan to Khartoum. Ethiopia has a royal family, which includes Queen Candace. You may know that Candace is not a personal name as in your country, but a dynastic title. So you would probably refer to her as the Queen Mother. In Ethiopia she rules the country on behalf of her son, the king, who is treated by the people as being in a special relationship to their deity, in a way which is thought to make it inappropriate for him to deal with secular matters. All this underlines the fact that Queen Candace is a prominent lady, but my concern is with one of her important officials, who is in charge of her treasury; I presume you would call him the Chancellor of the Exchequer. Apparently, he is a eunuch.

As I mentioned, he was occupying his time reading

(aloud) some well known sections of our Jewish Scriptures, and I used these as an excellent introduction to tell him the good news about Jesus. He was obviously ready for the message; why else would I have been sent into the desert to minister to him?

On hearing my message, the Ethiopian eunuch was happy and ready to acknowledge Jesus as the Son of God and he made an open profession of this, right there in the desert, and was baptized. The last I saw of him, he was joyously continuing his journey south to his own country.

That excursion from Samaria to the desert taught me a great deal, and I now believe I understand the reason for the mission. But I needed to return to a more conventional evangelistic ministry and soon found myself in Azotus, from whence I travelled about preaching the gospel in the surrounding towns before I reached Caesarea, a port on the Mediterranean coast. There I decided to settle, together with my family. All this took place twenty years ago and I have been happy to remain in relative obscurity all these years, with a settled evangelistic ministry, ably supported by my daughters.

I did have a surprise visit a short while ago, when Paul and another well–known Christian by the name of Luke arrived. Yes, this was the same Paul that I referred to in connection with Stephen's death! In a way, it was an intriguing demonstration of the power of the gospel. Twenty years earlier, Paul (or Saul as he was then) was persecuting the church, and was effectively the reason for my move to Samaria. Now, here he was being entertained in my home in Caesarea on his way to Jerusalem. Interestingly, they still refer to me as 'one of the seven', even after all these years!

8

Saul of Tarsus

I had the privilege of being born in a great city in a day of great cities. You must have heard of Tarsus. It can hold up its head with Athens, Corinth, Ephesus and the rest. It is a Greek city in the province of Cilicia, a meeting place of East and West, a busy metropolis with an impressive university. The city has half a million inhabitants. [Today it is a part of South East Turkey, tucked away in the top right hand corner of the Mediterranean.]

I had a privileged upbringing with strong influences from three cultures. The Greek influence was everywhere, of course, just as it was and is throughout the Roman Empire. Whatever your history books may say, the Greeks had conquered the world *culturally* and, in my day, even Rome was a Greek–speaking city. My contemporaries made much of that —I less so. We were, of course, under the dominion of Rome—as part of the great Roman Empire—but that was not a threat to me, since I was a

Roman citizen, something I inherited from my Father — quite a privilege! As a Roman, I had a Roman name, Paulus. But I did not really consider myself a Greek or a Roman. I was a Hebrew, the son of Hebrew parents. I belonged to the elite of Israel: the tribe of Benjamin.

You may know that the tribe of Benjamin has always held a special place in the aristocracy of Israel. From this tribe came the first king, Saul, and you should not be too surprised, therefore, when I tell you that Saul was the Jewish name given to me by my parents. My father had a strong influence on my early life. As a family we used the Hebrew language at home. I was sent first to school and then to a workshop. I became a young scholar and I also became a tentmaker. This was not particularly unusual in my day. But when I reached the age of fourteen or so, it was decided that I should give the local university at Tarsus a miss and go instead to Jerusalem, to sit at the feet of Gamaliel, the leading rabbi of his day. From the beginning, I threw myself into my studies and soon became the leading scholar amongst my contemporaries. What I lacked in bodily presence and eloquence, I made up for with study, application and ruthless ambition. I endeavoured to be a zealous Jew, attempting to keep the Jewish law in as blameless a fashion as is humanly possible. You may not know it but, for the Jew, zeal is the greatest quality of the religious life, and I *was* zealous! A distinguished career awaited me.

My Jewish upbringing and aspirations were clearly important influences in my life, and these were already moulding my attitudes. For example, I faithfully followed the teaching of our Jewish Scriptures in the matter of the role and status of women, and some may, quite wrongly, have thought of me as a misogynist. I may also have been seen as being something of a Philistine in matters of culture —paying insufficient heed to the beauties of nature and the attractions of art; someone with an all but complete indifference to the classical traditions of Greece. There is some truth in this. What I saw in Athens, for example, was a city full of idols; the great architectural masterpieces left me cold.

So there I was, in Jerusalem, somewhat precocious and strong–willed, the leading scholar in the school of Gamaliel, highly ambitious and zealous for the traditions of the fathers, 'a Hebrew of the Hebrews', and as far as outward righteousness is concerned, I do not think anyone could have found fault with me.

This brings me to the encounter that was to change everything. When I first heard of Jesus of Nazareth, someone a few years older than myself, from the backwaters of Galilee, the matter was a *minor* irritant. I knew that itinerant preachers were thick on the ground at the time, and I felt that this Jesus would soon go the way of the others. And this did indeed seem to happen. The events are well documented. One of his own number betrayed him, he was tried by the Roman procurator, Pontius Pilate, and to cut a long story short, he was crucified between two thieves. Now for me, at the time, that was that. My Scriptures told me that anyone dying on a cross was under the curse of God, and that seemed a fitting end for an anti establishment troublemaker!

Then his pathetic band of followers began declaring that the tomb was empty; that Jesus had been raised from the dead and was alive! I was not amused. How could God at one and the same time curse someone and then bring him back to life again? Absurd! The whole nonsense needed to be stamped out, and three things came together to set me up as an obvious candidate to apply the coup de grâce: my relative youth, (I was in my late twenties at the time); my strong pharisaic convictions, which this man had so offended; and my zealous ambition, which was looking for expression, for an outlet. So I set about the task with vigour. There was one obstacle, however. It was not only plebeian Galileans who were being taken in; priests and scholars were also being carried away. Even my former teacher, Gamaliel, would not come down off the fence.

One Hellenistic Jew, in particular, was a particular thorn in my side. His name was Stephen. There was something disturbing about him, and he possessed logical power, to boot. He was preaching about Jesus of Nazareth as the Righteous One, whose coming had been predicted by the prophets, and whom we had rejected as they had been rejected. Naturally I took a strong stand against his message. When the crunch came, I was in the thick of it. I not only consented to Stephen's death, I also held the clothes of those who did the actual stoning. But, I have to tell you, the whole experience left me feeling ill at ease.

Stephen's death raised as many questions as it answered. He went to his death with what I can only call a supernatural peace and, yes, glory —his face seemed to shine like an angel. How could it be? I pondered. The fellow was not an ignorant savage like some of them; he was a cultured Greek who clearly seemed to know the Jewish Scriptures. So he must have known that God had put a curse on Jesus? So was I missing something? You see, whether or not Jesus of Nazareth merited death was of minor importance; the fact that he did die on a cross was what really mattered, and this seemed to prove one thing decisively —that he could not be the Messiah!

So there followed a strange turmoil of mind; a mingling of anger, annoyance, amazement, perplexity and mental questionings. Something about Stephen lingered in my mind and I could not banish it. What was I to do? What would you have done? I followed a fairly obvious course of action: I kicked against the goad, trying to convince myself that I was right. I redoubled my efforts to stamp out the heresy. So I created even greater havoc amongst these so-called Christians, to the extent that I became their number one opponent.

I was extremely zealous. I did some horrible things. I tortured them to make them curse Jesus, and I imprisoned them. When they were being condemned to death, I cast my vote against them. So incensed was I that I took my campaign outside Jerusalem, outside Judea even, to all the surrounding countries —anywhere Jews were calling themselves Christians. Do not forget that in my day a writ from the high priest was respected by synagogues in other territories. The Romans allowed this —for a quiet life. So, to cut a long and painful story short, I obtained papers from the high priest to carry on the mayhem in Syria. Now Damascus, the capital of Syria, is around two hundred and twenty kilometres north of Jerusalem, and we had to make the journey on foot. So it took the best part of a week. I was accompanied by some officers from the Sanhedrin —a kind of Jewish police force.

We were getting close to Damascus. It was around midday. I shall never forget what followed! A light shone which was even brighter than the sun. We fell to the ground and I heard a voice, which said: "Saul! Saul! Why do you persecute me?"

"Who are you, Lord?" I asked.

"I am Jesus, whom you are persecuting," he replied. "Now get up and go into the city, and you will be told what you must do." He also said, "I have appeared to you to appoint you as a servant and as a witness of what you have seen of me and what I will show you. I will rescue you from your own people and from the Gentiles. I am sending you to them to open their eyes and turn them from darkness to light."[1]

Those who were with me heard the voice, but they did not see anyone. They quickly recovered, but I was left without my sight. In fact, my companions had to lead me into the city like a little child. The strangeness of all this is obvious, but my heart and mind had been prepared, and the events which followed confirmed that Jesus himself had appeared to me in an amazing way, changed me and set my life on a new course.

A Christian called Ananias came to see me. He obviously knew all about me and what had happened. He placed his hands on me and said, "Brother Saul, the Lord—Jesus, who appeared to you on the road as you were coming here—has sent me so that you may see again and be filled with the Holy Spirit." I regained my sight and was baptized in water. Then I took some food, and I quickly regained my strength. You see, I had not eaten for three days.

That was a dramatic time, for sure, but in one sense it was not the 'beginning'. The encounter with Jesus had begun sometime earlier, when, through his followers, I had been confronted by his claims, which I had been so violently opposing. Nor was it the *end*. Here was a life changing experience which was to completely alter everything: my whole outlook, my friends, my purpose in life —in other words, *my whole future*.

Above all, what changed was my relationship with God. I had met the risen Lord Jesus Christ and I could never be the same again. God, who first ordered light to shine out of the darkness, had flooded my heart with his light. But I now had some unlearning to do. You do not as a rule suddenly change from being an enemy of someone to being one of their most devoted followers. That process can require instruction or meditation on the word of God or direct revelation. In my case, after some discussion with Ananias, I had to get away to Arabia —not for days or weeks or even months, but for all of three years. I did not confer with any other Christians during that time. It had to be a long protracted encounter between myself and God in solitude. It was not cities or colleges or men or books that moulded my new thinking; it was God himself.

You see, when you become a Christian, when you truly encounter Christ, all problems do not suddenly disappear. In my case, I still believed that anyone dying on a cross was under the curse of God, and I needed to square this up with the fact that I now believed Jesus to be alive again. After much meditation, there was a direct revelation from God. I was shown that I had also been under the curse of God, because, like everyone else, I could not perfectly keep the law; and Jesus, the sinless one, had taken my curse when he died on the cross. He became a curse for me. He died, the just for the unjust, so that he could bring me (and many others) to God.

All that striving after perfection and law–keeping had been useless. This new relationship was all about grace —God's unmerited favour. And the cross, which had been such a stumbling block to me, I now knew to have been been the means of my salvation!

This learning process went on. I had been taught in the school of Gamaliel. Now I was being schooled in the Way of Christ. I realized that no-one is too bad to receive forgiveness, if he will repent and come to Christ. If he could redeem me, the chief of sinners, the persecutor of the church, then he could redeem anyone! Nor is anyone too good to need to repent. When I weighed up all my religious advantages, all my perceived goodness, they counted for nothing, compared with the excellency of knowing Christ.

What a learning time that was – and I left with a fire in my belly, waiting to tell everyone the good news —Jews and Gentiles alike. But after a few opportunities I was encouraged to go back to Cilicea, and I had to learn a lot of patience, which was quite a struggle for a headstrong convert like myself.

It was almost a decade later that, with Barnabas, I was chosen by the Holy Spirit to undertake a mission, which was to become my life's work. I became a missionary, and the Christian message was taken to many of the great cities of the Roman Empire. The names roll off the tongue: Ephesus, Philippi, Corinth, Athens and even Rome, and the Christian gospel spread like a fire! Within the space of ten years or so, much of the gentile world of Europe and Asia was touched by the gospel.

So here I am, aged sixty or so. Throughout my Christian life I have considered knowing Christ as everything. Now, looking back, I believe I have fought a good fight. I have finished the course; I have kept the faith and I am now ready to meet the Lord. That, in a nutshell, is my story.

TWO FINAL WORDS OF ENCOURAGEMENT

I want to leave with you two thoughts that come out of my decades of Christian experience and witness. The first is simply this: Jesus Christ is King of kings and Lord of lords, and all things were created by him and for him. He is supreme —the image of the invisible God. So to treat him as an optional extra is to deny him. In him all the fullness of God lives in bodily form.[2] Be encouraged, because through the gospel, Jesus has opened up to us a life that is eternal. So do not be ashamed of the gospel. Do not be ashamed of Christ. Give him your allegiance, because a day is coming when every knee is going to bow before him, and everyone is going to have to acknowledge him as Lord. Remember that Christ is all that matters, and when you look at any attributes you may have, any gifts, any privileges—anything which you thought was to your profit—you will be able to say with me, '...Whatever was to my profit, I now consider loss for the sake of Christ. What is more, I consider everything a loss compared to the surpassing greatness of knowing Christ Jesus my Lord....'[3]

The second thing I want to leave with you is something that I want to address specifically to those who would like to regard themselves as active, fervent Christians. It is this: God has a plan for your life. I hear some mutterings at this point: 'he doesn't know me; he doesn't know my circumstances, my difficulties, my doubts.' Let me say it again: God has a plan for your life. In all things, God *does* work for the good of those who love him.[4] Believe it! You talk of hardships and setbacks. Allow me to tell you a thing or two about my own experiences. Right at the beginning, there in Damascus, the town governor sent men to arrest me. I only escaped by climbing through a window and being let down from the city walls in a basket. And since then? Well I know much about the inside of prison cells; I have been beaten times without number. I have received the regulation thirty nine stripes on five occasions. I have been stoned; I have been shipwrecked; I have spent twenty four hours in the open sea. I have faced constant danger. I have known exhaustion, pain, hunger and thirst. But I say to you: '...we are more than conquerors through him who loved us. For I am convinced that neither death nor life, neither angels nor demons, neither the present nor the future, nor any powers, neither height nor depth, nor anything else in all creation, will be able to separate us from the love of God that is in Christ Jesus our Lord.'[5] Trust him; place all your hope in him.

Yes —like me, sometimes you will need to learn patience. You may also have to deal with things which can be hard to understand. I have had a thorn in the flesh for much of my life. On three occasions I have particularly asked the Lord to take it from me. Do you know what his response has been? —"My grace is sufficient for you, for my power is made perfect in weakness."[6] The 'thorn' remains to this day.

The treasure that God has given us is in 'jars of clay', to show that the power is from him not from ourselves.[7] At the moment, you may feel hard-pressed on every side, but be encouraged —'though outwardly we are wasting away, yet inwardly we are being renewed day by day. For our light and momentary troubles are achieving for us an eternal glory that far outweighs them all.'[8]

A PRAYER[9]

For this reason I kneel before the Father, from whom his whole family in heaven and on earth derives its name. I pray that out of his glorious riches he may strengthen you with power through his Spirit in your inner being, so that Christ may dwell in your hearts through faith. And I pray that you, being rooted and established in love, may have power, together with all the saints, to grasp how wide and high and long and deep is the love of Christ, and to know this love that surpasses knowledge—that you may be filled to the measure of all the fullness of God.

Now to him who is able to do immeasurably more than all we ask or imagine, according to his power that is at work within us, to him be glory in the church and in Christ Jesus throughout all generations, for ever and ever!

Amen

9

Cornelius the Centurion

Here I am, living in this pleasant place. I love the natural beauty, the blue sea, the sunsets, the harbour, and the climate. Yes, I can think of worse places to be!

As you know, this is not where I was born or bred, and sometimes I do feel like a stranger in a foreign land. Looking back, and trying to be realistic, I cannot help feeling that I have not fulfilled all my potential, but I do know that, with God's help, I have accomplished something —better to be a good *centurion* than a bad *tribune*!

I was born in Italy and I have been a Roman soldier all my working life. Today, I am serving in what is called the 'Italian Regiment'. Some years ago, we were posted to Caesarea, on the Mediterranean coast. As postings go, it had pros and cons. A garrison city, named after Augustus Caesar, it has a distinctly Roman flavour. As the administrative capital of the province of Judea, it possesses many of the features of any Roman city. It has its amphitheatre, market, temple to Augustus, fine streets and houses, fountains and aqueduct, to say nothing of the splendid artificial harbour, built by the Jewish king, Herod the Great. We are very much a police force in this seat of Roman government. It is here that the procurator is based. You must have heard of one of them — Pontius Pilate. He was in control here for ten years, and his term of office ended only two years ago. In many ways, Pilate was the archetypal Roman, with an intriguing mixture of courage, guile and cowardice. You may have heard of his part in the trial and crucifixion of someone called Jesus of Nazareth? That was about six years ago.

There is a constant tension and mistrust between we Romans and the local people. No love is lost either way. The Jews for their part are, of course, a very exclusive people. We Romans, and any other so-called Gentiles for that matter, are certainly not welcome. We are not even allowed to cross the threshold of a Jewish home!

In the Roman army, I have risen to the rank of centurion, and I need to explain where that fits into the general scheme of things. You will have heard of Roman legions. These consist of ten so-called cohorts, each of which is commanded by a tribune. Each cohort consists of six centuries (i.e. six groups of a hundred soldiers) and each century is under the command of a centurion. It has long been felt that we centurions form the solid backbone of the Roman army. Let me read to you a statement of what is expected of us:

Centurions should not be overbold and reckless, so much as good leaders; of steady and prudent mind, not prone to take the offensive, to start fighting wantonly; but able, when overwhelmed and hard pressed, to stand fast and die at their post.

I have always tried to live up to these laudable aspirations—to the best of my ability.

I am sure you will know something of the lifestyle of the typical Roman soldier; much of it is not very flattering. At least, that was my view, and when I came to Caesarea, I became disillusioned. I was disgusted with the excesses of paganism. There had to be more to life than that! So I became attracted to the religion and beliefs of the local residents, the Jews, who were so despised by most of my colleagues. I do not know what really attracted me. Maybe it was their noble doctrine of one God —Yahweh. Maybe it was the purity of their morality, the sanctity of home life. It could have been their magnificent and incomparable literature (even to someone well versed in the works of Roman and Greek writers). Certainly, I was moved by their majestic worship.

I found myself drawn more and more to the Jewish religion, eventually becoming a convert. The Jews themselves talked of me as a *God fearer*. I attended the synagogue, as the Jews did. I gave alms to the people, as many of the Jews did; I had a disciplined prayer life, as the Jews did. You may rightly feel that I lived, acted and prayed like a Jew. But here is the crunch —*to the Jews*, I was still a Gentile and therefore an alien from the commonwealth of Israel and a stranger from the covenants of promise. I had not submitted to various aspects of their Law, particularly circumcision, and this ruled me out, so far as they were concerned; although many of them were very kind and spoke highly of me to their friends. But they dared not come into my house, and

I was certainly forbidden from entering their homes! So, although I can honestly say that I was, and still am, of good report amongst the Jews, the gulf between us was great. In one sense, that did not matter, because, after all, religion is a personal thing. Indeed, to the outsider, I may have appeared outwardly fulfilled, and it is certainly true that I did receive much succour from my new religion, as did my family, my household and some of my soldier colleagues. But hear me on this! There was a deep longing within me for something more, something deeper and more fulfilling. In my prayer time, I would often cry out with Job, "O that I may know where I might find him"!

Then I began to hear of this Jesus of Nazareth, who had been crucified by us, some six or so years earlier. The so-called "followers of the Way" were boldly proclaiming that, three days after the crucifixion, Jesus had been raised from the dead, and that he was now very much alive. Apparently, after ascending to heaven, he supernaturally empowered his followers to preach the new faith. I gleaned this from some of his disciples who were residing in Caesarea. Prominent in this group was someone called Philip the Evangelist. Philip had settled here, following an itinerant ministry in Samaria and other places.

So, a short while ago, I found myself in deep need. I was completely alienated from the more perverse aspects of my Roman past; I was receiving some comfort from the religion of the Jews but, in all honesty, there was still a deep hunger for something more. I heard that when Jesus was on earth he had talked of the kingdom of God as being like a merchant looking for fine pearls who, when he found a very valuable one, sold everything he had and bought it. I can truthfully say that, for some time, I had been seeking goodly pearls —though I did not yet have the pearl of great value. At that time, though, what I could do was to *pray* to the God of Israel. I am delighted to tell you that my prayers were answered in a most miraculous way. My immediate family, my household and some of my soldier colleagues were similarly blessed.

This is what happened. On one of those days when I was free to pray at the recognized three o'clock slot, I saw a being whom I knew was an angel. There was no vagueness or uncertainty about this —I *saw* him distinctly. A soldier is not expected to be fearful, but I have to admit to experiencing fear that day! This is what the angel said to me: "Your prayers and gifts to the poor have come up as a memorial offering before God. Now send men to Joppa to bring back a man called Simon who is called Peter. He is staying with Simon the tanner, whose house is by the sea."[1]

The message was certainly very specific. So I called together two of my servants and a God–fearing soldier, and I explained to them what had happened, then sent them on their way —to Joppa, which is about fifty kilometres south on the coast road which passes through Caesarea, on its way from Acco in the north to Joppa in the south.

I subsequently learned that similar miraculous events were taking place in Joppa —in the home of the tanner I was told about by the heavenly messenger. I need to explain these things to you, and the background. Simon Peter, who was arguably the closest of all the disciples to Jesus of Nazareth, was staying in the home of a tanner, which is, in itself, interesting. Tanners work with dead animals, in order to convert their skins into leather, and the Jews regard this as 'unclean'. By staying in the home of Simon, Peter was therefore disregarding the restriction —a clear indication of an emancipation in Peter's attitude to at least some of the regulations of the Jewish law. But a far more radical challenge was awaiting him! Peter's experience was to be somewhat different from mine, though it was complementary. It was noon on the day after my encounter with the heavenly messenger. Peter was very hungry. Lunch was being prepared, and he fell into a trance, in which he was shown by the Lord something very significant: that he was no longer bound by Jewish dietary regulations. Then, as he was still thinking about that vision, the Spirit said to him, "Simon, three men are looking for you. So get up and go downstairs. Do not hesitate to go with them for I have sent them."[2]

So Peter went downstairs, told the strangers he was the one they were looking for and asked them why they had come. Then he invited them into the tanner's home to be his guests —yet another indication of emancipation on Peter's part: entertaining non–Jews!

Anyway, having exchanged their astonishing stories, on the following day the group began the journey back to Caesarea: my colleagues, Peter and *six* of his friends — other believers. Peter was wise enough to take with him the requisite number of witnesses for any future discussions or issues that might arise with other church leaders. The group finally reached Caesarea four days after I had first seen the angel. Not surprisingly, I had detailed knowledge of their likely time of arrival in Caesarea, and when they reached my home it was filled with my relatives and close friends, all eagerly awaiting Peter's arrival. It was three o'clock in the afternoon and, after some pleasantries, Peter addressed us. He first explained how his attitude had been transformed, and how he was now happy to enter the home of a non-Jew to explain the message of Jesus. You can imagine the sense of anticipation as we settled down to listen to Peter. He began by emphasising the basic facts about Jesus, with which, of course, we were already conversant. He said, "You know the message God sent to the people of Israel, telling the good news of peace through Jesus Christ, who is Lord of all. You know what has happened throughout Judea, beginning in Galilee after the baptism that John preached — how God anointed Jesus of Nazareth with the Holy Spirit and power, and how he went around doing good and healing all who were under the power of the devil, because God was with him. We are witnesses of everything he did in the country of the Jews and in Jerusalem. They killed him by hanging him on a tree, but God raised him from the dead on the third day and caused him to be seen. He was not seen by all the people but by witnesses whom God had already chosen—by us who ate and drank with him after he rose from the dead. He commanded us to preach to the people and to testify that he is the one whom God appointed as judge of the living and the dead. All the prophets testify about him that everyone who believes in him receives forgiveness of sins through his name."[3]

Peter said other things of course, but that was the heart of his message. It was made abundantly clear that all the good deeds, all the prayers, all the alms, any kindness to neighbours and colleagues, however commendable they might have been, were not sufficient for salvation —which could not be earned. To be saved we needed faith; we needed to believe the good news of Jesus.

Our hearts were soon responding to Jesus. He was

clearly the 'something more' that we longed for. What he had done on the cross was of far greater value than all our good deeds!

Then something amazing happened. As Peter was speaking, a deep sense of the presence of God came over the meeting; our hearts were warmed; we were lost in wonder and worship. Quite spontaneously, we began to respond by speaking in other, heavenly, languages, and we felt an irresistible urge to praise God. It was awesome! Peter's sermon came to an abrupt halt, but we were to learn of the significance *for us* of the words of Jesus to the first disciples, after he had been raised from the dead: "John baptised with water, but... you will be baptised with the Holy Spirit."[4] We had clearly been baptized with the Holy Spirit, just as the disciples and others had been on that day of Pentecost, which followed soon after Jesus had ascended to heaven. It was clear that God was giving the same gift of the Holy Spirit to both Jewish and Gentile believers. On that momentous day, we had been given repentance into life! By grace, our hearts were purified! We had experienced the infilling and empowering of the Holy Spirit!

To confirm and seal what had happened to us, Peter baptised us in water, as Jesus had commanded. For our part, we asked Peter to stay with us for a few extra days. We realized that what had happened to us was just the beginning, and that we needed instruction and fellowship.

Do you know what I am talking about? Have you believed? Have you been baptised in the Holy Spirit? Peter often reminded us that the promise was not only for us and our children, but also for those who are far off — for all whom God calls!

Although we did not realize it at the time, the events

that afternoon in my home in Caesarea, were to have an enormous impact on the whole church and its outreach ministry. Peter would often use my experience, and that of other Gentiles, to convince sceptical colleagues. He declared of us: "God, who knows the heart, showed that he accepted them by giving the Holy Spirit to them, just as he did to us. He made no distinction between us and them, for he purified their hearts by faith."[5]

SOME VERSES FROM THE EPISTLES

Therefore, remember that formerly you, who are Gentiles by birth.... were separate from Christ, excluded from citizenship in Israel and foreigners to the covenants of promise, without hope and without God in the world. But now in Christ Jesus you who were once far away have been brought near through the blood of Christ.[6]

Consequently, you are no longer foreigners and aliens, but fellow–citizens with God's people and members of God's household.[7]

There is neither Jew nor Greek, slave nor free, male nor female, for you are all one in Christ Jesus.[8]

10

Silas

I am writing from Rome. I am with one of the original disciples of Jesus of Nazareth, Simon Peter. Being here is less of a problem for me than it is for him, simply because I am a Roman citizen.

I have been helping Peter to write a letter to Christians, mainly Jewish Christians, who were driven out of Jerusalem by persecution and scattered throughout Asia. As I have done so, I have been reminiscing. We go back a long way, over three decades in fact —to the time when Jesus of Nazareth was crucified and was raised from the dead on the third day. Peter and I were both members of the young church in Jerusalem. It was all very Jewish in those days, of course. Again, this was no problem for me, because I am a Jew. So I am like my friend and one-time companion, Paul, or Saul of Tarsus as he is sometimes known —a Jew, but at the same time a Roman citizen; and I am a Christian! Silvanus is my Roman name, but I am better known by my Jewish name, Silas. The story I want to share with you really begins after the gospel had spread into Gentile territory, when Antioch was rivalling Jerusalem as a centre of Christian influence. Here is the background.

After the resurrection of Jesus, and following the birth of the church on the day of Pentecost, the gospel spread throughout Jerusalem and the surrounding area. However, it took time to fulfil the express command of Jesus that it should reach nearby Samaria. In fact it required persecution to bring that about. So, by one means or another, the gospel was extending its influence. Before long, the church had to face up to the challenge of non-Jews becoming Christians. With difficulty, we safely negotiated that, with significant help from my present companion, Simon Peter. He had an amazing encounter with a Roman centurion called Cornelius, who was based at the time in Caesarea on the Mediterranean coast. Cornelius was one of the first Gentile Christians.

As I have indicated, slowly but surely the centre of influence moved from Jerusalem to Antioch, a large and important city some four hundred kilometres to the north.

Church growth was now dramatic, especially amongst the Gentiles, and the spread of the gospel seemed inexorable. Paul was very much involved in these developments and it seemed that nothing could hinder the work of preaching the good news. Then, ten years after the conversion of Cornelius, came a crisis. Some bigoted Jews travelled to Antioch and wanted to insist that Gentile Christians had to adhere to all the laws of Moses, including the one concerning circumcision. They were willing for Gentiles to be admitted to the church, but only on condition that they first became Jews!

Certainly, to Paul and to many of the Antioch leaders,

this was unthinkable, and, if the Jerusalem church had insisted on the condition, a damaging split would have ensued. To put it bluntly, a Jewish Christian church based in Jerusalem, and a predominantly Gentile church in Antioch. So, to cut a long story short, Paul, together with one of his closest friends, Barnabas, went to have it out with the leaders of the Jerusalem church. They made the long journey to Jerusalem, and what followed has become popularly known as the Jerusalem Council. I have seen an account of the council events written by one of my closest friends, Luke. Certainly, it is factually correct, but it gives scant reference to the strong feelings and tensions of the time. These were felt on both sides of the dispute, especially by Paul. However, reason and Christian charity prevailed, and a letter was written which had the agreement of all. This is what it said:

The apostles and elders, your brothers,
To the Gentile believers in Antioch, Syria and Cilicia:
Greetings!

We have heard that some went out from us, without our authorization and disturbed you, troubling your minds by what they said. So we all agreed to choose some men and send them to you, with our dear friends Barnabas and Paul— men who have risked their lives for the name of our Lord Jesus Christ.

Therefore we are sending Judas and Silas to confirm by word of mouth what we are writing. It seemed good to the Holy Spirit and to us not to burden you with anything beyond the following requirements: You are to abstain from foods sacrificed to idols, from blood, from the meat of strangled animals and from sexual immorality. You will do well to avoid these things.

Farewell! [1]

Now the council's action was very wise. Had Paul and Barnabas gone back alone, their words could have been questioned. A letter by itself could have been seen as cold and impersonal. But, hopefully, my presence and that of Judas Barsabbas added a note of warmth and authenticity.

This is the point at which I became directly involved. I was asked by my Jerusalem colleagues to be one of the emissaries and I readily agreed. Little did I know at that time that it would mean a sea change in my Christian ministry, and it would be some time before I could even contemplate taking up again a leadership role in the Jerusalem church. Not that I am complaining! The subsequent events have been far from boring or uneventful, as I will attempt to show.

The letter we carried to Antioch had the desired effect and a damaging split was avoided. For a while, Judas and I exercised our prophetic ministry in the new sphere. But the time came for us to return to Jerusalem, and we went with the church's blessing and gratitude.

My movements at that time have been the subject of speculation. Some believe I immediately changed my mind and decided to stay at Antioch; others that, having travelled the long distance to Jerusalem, I almost immediately got the call to return to Antioch —something that involved a combined journey of over eight hundred kilometres. Sufficient to say that, by this time, I had struck up a close friendship with Paul and, when he had a serious disagreement with Barnabas over travel companions, he asked me to join him on a major missionary enterprise. I readily accepted, leaving Barnabas to go his own way with his cousin, John Mark.

I believe the local church at Antioch was not too pleased by the turn of events and, especially, the tensions, though they certainly gave their blessing to Paul and myself. They commended us to the grace of God and we went on our way, strengthening some of the churches in Asia which Paul had founded on his first missionary enterprise.

At Lystra, we came into contact with an interesting young fellow by the name of Timothy. His mother was Jewish, but his father was a Greek. He was an active Christian and well respected by his local church, and Paul asked him to join us on our travels. All three of us became close friends. From time to time, we were joined by a doctor called Luke, and the fellowship amongst all four of us was rich and warm, and the ministry very fruitful. By the way, Luke was taking copious notes, with the intention of providing a written account of our travels.

For some reason, which I might add we now fully understand, the Holy Spirit kept telling us not to venture into parts of Asia, so we proceeded to Troas, on the coast of the Aegean sea. You will probably know it better by its ancient name —Troy. It was there that Paul had his now famous Macedonian call. One night, he had a vision of a man begging him to 'Come over to Macedonia and help us.' We were happy to oblige, seeing the hand of God in the development. So the four of us set sail for Europe. The wind was with us and the journey took only two days. We landed in Neapolis, a port some twelve kilometres from the major city of the area —Philippi.

I need to tell you something about Philippi. It had been founded by Philip, the father of Alexander the Great. But it was now a Roman colony —though not a colony as you would know it. It had dignity; veteran Roman soldiers settled there. The inhabitants were intensely proud of their citizenship. So there it was. There was no more strategic site in the whole of Europe: Philippi, lying snugly in the hills that effectively divide Europe and Asia.

Paul is a wise leader. If he stays any length of time in one place, you can be sure that it has a strategic value. Whilst the stay in Philippi was not that long, it was significant. A number of events took place while we were there which graphically illustrate the growth of Christianity —the opportunities, the universal appeal, the opposition to be overcome, the weapons to be employed, the promise of ultimate victory.

There were not many Jews in Philippi —fewer than ten Jewish males, in fact. How do I know that? Well, there was no synagogue. Had at least ten Jewish men lived in the city, there would have been. In its place was a 'gathering for prayer', located some distance outside the gates of the city on the river bank. As was our custom, on the first Sabbath day we were in Philippi, we sought out the Jewish community at prayer time. Only women were present on that occasion.

We met an interesting lady by the name of Lydia. She hailed from Thyatira in Asia, a place well known for its purple dye which has to be gathered drop by drop from a shellfish and so is expensive! It is not too surprising that Lydia's business in Philippi involved dealings in purple cloth. She was clearly reasonably rich. She had obviously been much influenced by our Jewish faith and was a keen proselyte. It was clear to all of us that the Lord was touching her heart, and she responded to Paul's preaching. She was soundly converted and immediately began to witness to her family and household. Very soon, she was baptised, along with those close to her.

Lydia was a persuasive lady and she prevailed on us to stay at her home —and I do mean *prevailed*. So there we were in Philippi, staying in the home of a recently converted, wealthy, business lady. But, you may ask, what's so amazing about that, over and above the obvious fact that she was the first Christian convert on European soil? I will tell you. Before his conversion, Paul had been a Pharisee. In those days he would have repeated words like, 'O God, I thank you that I am neither a Gentile, nor a slave, nor a woman!' Do not forget that women are generally considered intellectually inferior, and they are often denied education. So it is possible to see a very significant development in our dealings with Lydia. Here was the gospel making a difference in social behaviour and relationships. Paul would often remind us that in Christ Jesus there is neither male nor female; we are all one in Christ Jesus. Paul was practising what he preached when he agreed to stay in the home of Lydia.

Keep that in mind as I tell you of the next amazing incident that occurred at Philippi, one which again involved a woman —this time, not a rich business lady, but a demon-possessed local girl.[2] I want you to attend carefully to this, because I believe it is important. Paul would often remind us that our struggle is not against flesh and blood, but against the spiritual forces of evil in the heavenly realm. We must never let Satan get an advantage over us. Happily, we are not ignorant of his devices, subtle and devious as these may be. If we ever needed reminding that we were in a battle, we were left in no doubt in Philippi. The young girl was, effectively, a slave to a group of unscrupulous men who were getting rich on her fortune–telling abilities. Now follow this closely. The demonised slave girl continually followed us, shouting out something that was basically true: "These men are servants of the Most High God, who are telling you the way to be saved." But Paul would have none of it, and you need to know why. Alliance with evil is a very subtle peril. If you admit the devil into the propagation of the gospel, he will soon distort what is taught, introducing heresy. Satan was defeated on the cross, but is still around for a season. We must resist him.

The whole matter so troubled Paul that he addressed the evil spirit: "In the name of Jesus Christ I command you to come out of her." Then the evil spirit left her. She later responded to the gospel message and was filled with the Holy Spirit.

So that was the first attack of the devil, and it was subtle. The second was more overt. When Paul exorcised the evil spirit, the girl's owners were incensed, seeing their livelihood disappear at a stroke. They seized us, told lies, and stirred up the people. The local magistrates got involved and ordered us to be stripped and beaten. We were severely flogged and then thrown into an inner prison. It was dark. It was dismal. Then, to add insult to injury, they put our feet in stocks. But know this— the devil is always defeated when he imprisons a Christian. Our moment of greatest exposure to the wiles of the devil was not when he had us imprisoned, but when he got the slave girl to shout out the truth about us. Satan, a defeated enemy, has some powers, but they are not unlimited, and he always overstretches himself when he puts Christians in jail.

The four of us have often debated why they took Paul and myself and left the others alone. This is what we think: Paul and I look like Jews, because we are Jews; Timothy is only half a Jew, and Luke looks like the Gentile he is. Their anger was against *Jews*, so it was only Paul and myself who suffered the beating and the imprisonment. I cannot tell you that the beatings and the prison cell were pleasant—of course not—but we have learnt to praise God in all circumstances, in sickness and in health, in the good times and the bad. So, come midnight, in that stinking jail, Paul and I began singing hymns and praying; not that our prayers were prayers of petition on this occasion. We were just caught up in adoration and worship. For me, it was one of the highlights of my Christian experience. God was so near, and the beatings and the discomfort were forgotten. You will be interested to learn that the other prisoners were not annoyed by our enthusiasm at such a late hour. As far as we could judge, they were listening to us with deep interest and good humour.

Anyway, Philippi was to witness another miracle that night. In the early hours of the morning there was an earthquake. Such timing was surely beyond all possibility of coincidence! The result was certainly miraculous. The prison doors opened, everybody's chains came loose, no-one was injured, no-one escaped. We stopped the jailer from committing suicide, and we led him to the Lord. Indeed, his whole household followed suit; they all believed on the Lord Jesus Christ and were all baptised at the same time as the jailer. So, mark this: a Roman jailer became a Christian. First there had been a business woman from the upper classes, then a poor slave girl, and now a middle class Roman! —men and women, rich and poor, from Asia, Macedonia and Rome. The Christian gospel is for *all*, and nowhere is this better seen than in our visit to Philippi.

Our stay in Philippi was relatively short, but its importance was far reaching, and a Christian church was founded that became very close to Paul's heart. From Philippi, we travelled to Thessalonica, before moving on to Berea. Paul then had an interesting visit to Athens, before Timothy and I met up with him again in Corinth. It was a time of rich fellowship, blessing and fruitfulness. But that was more than ten years ago, and here I am in Rome helping my old Jerusalem colleague, Simon Peter. The emperor, Nero, is flexing his muscles, and it looks as if we are in for a time of severe persecution.

Peter has told others that he regards me as 'a faithful brother', and I am so thankful to God for all my fellow believers. My closing words to you are these:

Respect those who work hard among you, who are over you in the Lord and who admonish you. Hold them in the highest regard in love because of their work. Live in peace with each other.... Warn those who are idle, encourage the timid, help the weak, be patient with everyone. Make sure that nobody pays back wrong for wrong, but always try to be kind to each other and to everyone else. Be joyful always; pray continually; give thanks in all circumstances, for this is God's will for you in Christ Jesus. Do not put out the Spirit's fire; do not treat prophecies with contempt. Test everything. Hold on to the good. Avoid every kind of evil.[3]

11

Apollos, Priscilla and Aquila

I, Paul, am in Rome, awaiting trial, but I can and do welcome those who come to my rented house to see me. Although this is a form of imprisonment, and therefore some of my liberties have been removed, I am still able to preach the kingdom of God and teach about the Lord Jesus Christ.[1]

With much time on my hands, I have been able to reminisce about all the exciting developments that have taken place since I first became a Christian close on thirty five years ago. My thoughts have turned to those special days when we first took the gospel to major cities like Corinth and Ephesus. I vividly recall the advances which took place at that time, about fifteen years or so ago. I am happy to put on record my indebtedness to my co–workers. Here, I want to single out for special mention Apollos, Priscilla and Aquila.

Apollos is certainly the most well known of the three. and he is a man of many talents.[2] He is a Jew, from

Alexandria in Egypt. You may know that there are close on a million Jews in Alexandria, almost half the total population of that great city. In many ways, Alexandria is the second city in the Roman Empire, after Rome itself of course. It has a university and is the centre of Greek learning. Apollos himself is an educated man, with a thorough knowledge of the Scriptures. Indeed, he has sometimes been described as being 'an eloquent man and mighty in the Scriptures.'

When I first got to hear about Apollos, who moved to Ephesus, it was clear that he had been well instructed in the way of the Lord; he also spoke with great fervour and taught about Jesus accurately. But in those early days there was something missing. I can sum it up by saying that, at that time, Apollos 'knew only the baptism of John'. Certainly, he had not been baptised in the Holy Spirit, as the disciples of Jesus had been on that famous day of Pentecost.

I can attest that this deficiency was also apparent amongst some of the disciples in Ephesus where Apollos had been teaching. You will know that I have spent a considerable amount of time there, and, on the occasion of my longest visit to that city, I met a group of twelve disciples. They were certainly open to God, but I asked them a question: "Did you receive the Holy Spirit when you believed?" They replied that they had not even heard that there is a Holy Spirit. So I continued, saying, "Then what baptism did you receive?"

They replied, "John's baptism."

They were sincere and honest, and there were the signs of ascetism and the outward signs of repentance—all the marks of John's baptism, in fact—but something was certainly missing. I explained that John's baptism was a baptism of repentance and that he had told the people to believe in the one coming after him —Jesus. So they were baptised into the name of the Lord Jesus; then I placed my hands on them, the Holy Spirit came on them, and they spoke in tongues and prophesied.

Apollos himself was to have a similar experience. I was not involved on that occasion. Rather, it was my co–workers Priscilla and Aquila. The details must wait until I tell you something about this husband and wife team. Nearly twenty years after the birth of the Christian church, the mad Roman Emperor Claudius expelled Jews from Rome. Some believe that his wrath was really focussed on the new sect of Christians rather than the Jews in general, but, be that as it may, it is certainly true that Aquila and Priscilla were expelled from Rome at that time. By then they were both Christians (as well as being Jews). The couple moved to Corinth, and that is where I first met them. They were tentmakers by trade and Corinth was an obvious move for them, given the circumstances. As a major seaport and trade centre, it was alive with activity and business opportunities —an ideal place for them to continue their tentmaking business.

Some time after their arrival in Corinth, I also journeyed to the city and resided with them during my stay there. As the three of us were Christians and tentmakers, the arrangement seemed an obvious one. We developed a close and lasting Christian friendship, and the couple were a constant source of encouragement to me, not only in Corinth, but also in subsequent journeys which we all undertook.

Aquila and Priscilla, as a matter of fact, are noted for their travelling. Let me explain. I know that Aquila is a native of Pontus and I assume that his wife came from the same area. Pontus is an Asian province, bordering on what you would know as the Black Sea. It happens to be well known as a centre of activity in tentmaking, which probably explains their interest in that trade. From Pontus they had moved to Rome, only to be expelled by Claudius. They moved to Corinth, where I first met them. When I left Corinth for Ephesus, I took Aquila and Priscilla with me. However, for me, this particular visit was brief and I soon set sail for Caesarea on the Mediterranean coast. I left the couple behind and they continued to be very helpful to the Christians there. In fact Christians in Ephesus used to meet in their house.

Now Claudius died six years after he expelled the Jews from Rome, to be succeeded by the Emperor Nero, and this opened up the way for Priscilla and Aquila to return to Rome. There they continued to host a house church and they continued to be a great encouragement to me. In fact, they risked their lives for me on one occasion. You would have thought that they deserved a settled existence after all the travelling —but no! They left Rome for Ephesus again and now, some twenty or so years after the Claudius expulsion, they are back ministering in Ephesus. I do sometimes wonder if their wanderings have finally ceased, but somehow I do not think so!

Now I can tell you something of the amazing contact between them and Apollos, but I should mention first that, for one reason or another, contact between myself and Apollos has been elusive. It was many years before we were able to meet face to face and share in the ministry together. You will recall that I mentioned leaving Priscilla and Aquila in Ephesus, while I sailed to Caesarea. During my absence they interacted with Apollos and he then proceeded to Corinth with the church's blessing. As soon as he left, I returned to Ephesus. (I did point out that contact between him and myself had been elusive! — though even at that time we saw ourselves as being sharers together of the ministry and we did meet sometime later.)

So let me turn to that contact between Apollos, Aquila and Priscilla in Ephesus. As I mentioned, at this time Apollos knew only the baptism of John, like those disciples I met in Ephesus. I can only assume that Priscilla and Aquila listened with increasing concern to Apollos speaking, until one day they took him aside and invited him to their home. Their strong desire was to explain the way of God to him more adequately. To his great credit, Apollos accepted the invitation and responded to their teaching. There is much to be learnt from the interaction of Apollos with Aquila and Priscilla which took place then.

It would be a great mistake to think that being tentmakers made the couple somehow inferior intellectually! Moreover, I know nothing that would indicate that Priscilla was in any way inferior to her husband in matters of culture and intellect. Having conceded that, it is at the same time certainly true that they were confronting one of the most impressive and intelligent preachers in the young church. This was the situation they had to deal with. There was Apollos, a Jew from Alexandria, talented, eloquent, impressive, but lacking one vital spiritual ingredient. And there they were —knowing the truth of God more accurately in at least one or two vitally important areas. As the couple ministered to Apollos, they needed and were given quite extraordinary wisdom, tact, courage and love. Apollos, for his part, needed extraordinary modesty and godliness, to receive in humility the ministry that was being given. There is a fine line between criticism and advice, for sure, but through this contact the church was strengthened. One thing is clear —following that meeting, the ministry of Apollos became one of even greater power and fruitfulness. When he moved on to Corinth, he was a great help to the Christians, vigorously refuting the Jews in public debate and proving conclusively from the Scriptures that Jesus was the Christ.

Some of the Christians at Corinth responded to his ministry by wanting to link themselves particularly with his name. Of course, he was not alone in noticing that tendency amongst certain believers, since others wanted to say 'I follow Paul', and others wished to treat Peter in a similar way. I pointed out that there is error in this worldly, immature way of thinking, when I wrote this to them: 'What, after all, is Apollos? And what is Paul? Only servants, through whom you came to believe — as the Lord has assigned to each his task. I planted the seed. Apollos watered it, but God made it grow. So neither he who plants nor he who waters is anything, but only God, who makes things grow. The man who plants and the man who waters have one purpose, and each will be rewarded according to his own labour. For we are God's fellow-workers; you are God's field, God's building.... So then, no more boasting about men! All things are yours, whether Paul or Apollos or Cephas or the world or life or death or the present or the future —all are yours, and you are of Christ, and Christ is of God.'[3]

NOTES

See the following passages (NIV).

Chapter One

[1] Isaiah 40:3–5.
[2] Mark 1:7–8.
[3] Luke 3:14.
[4] Mark 1:11.
[5] Isaiah 53.
[6] Mark 6:18.
[7] Matthew 9:14.
[8] Matthew 11:3.
[9] John 1:6–8.

Chapter Two

[1] John 18:29.
[2] John 18:31.
[3] Luke 23:2.
[4] John 18:36.
[5] Luke 23:5.
[6] John 19:12.
[7] Acts 2:22ff.

Chapter Three

[1] Acts 1:12ff.
[2] Acts 2:1–4.
[3] Acts 2:14.

Chapter Four

[1] Acts 3:14–15a.
[2] Acts 3:13bff.
[3] Psalm 118:22–23.
[4] Isaiah 53:1–6.
[5] Galatians 3:13.

Chapter Five

[1] Acts 5:35b–39.

Chapter Six

[1] 2 Timothy 4:11.

Chapter Seven

[1] Acts 7:51bf.

Chapter Eight

[1] Acts 9:4–5 and 26:12ff.
[2] Colossians 1 and 2:9.
[3] Philippians 3:7–8.
[4] Romans 8:28.
[5] Romans 8:37ff.
[6] 2 Corinthians 12:9.
[7] 2 Corinthians 4:7.
[8] 2 Corinthians 4:16–17.
[9] Ephesians 3:14–20.